Easy Heirloom Embroidery

CHERYL FALL

Published by

KRAUSE PUBLICATIONS
700 E. State St.
Iola, WI 54990-0001
Telephone 715-445-2214
www.krause.com

Please call or write for our free catalog. Our toll-free number to place an order or obtain a free catalog is 800-258-0929 or please use our regular business telephone 715-445-2214 for editorial comment and further information.

Library of Congress Catalog Number 2001086342
ISBN 0-87349-229-3

Dedication

This book is dedicated to all of the people out there who are willing to pick up a needle and learn something new, to use their own two hands to create something beautiful and develop new skills. I hope embroidery becomes your main obsession!

Table of Contents

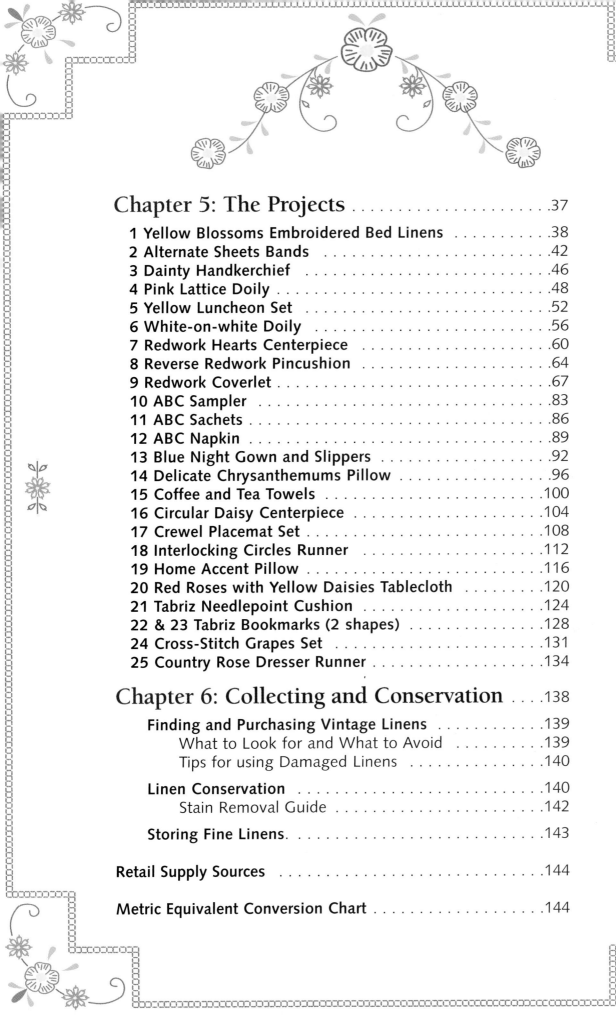

Acknowledgments

The author would like to thank the following companies and individuals for their help in creating this book. It's nice to have such a terrific support network!

Krause Publications
Tracy Schmidt and Maria Turner and the rest of the crew—thanks for having patience with me when things got "hairy."

Zweigart
Jim Kornecki
Their gorgeous fabrics grace nearly every project featured in this book.

Coats & Clark / Anchor
Meta Hoge, Dennis Yelen, Lori Tarantini, Kathleen Sams and Martha Goodlet—their selection of threads, floss, pearl cotton and tapestry wool never stopped flowing.

DMC
Jill Reed Siroty and Vicky Wells—they too provided many of the threads, pearl cotton and wools used in this book

And to my family…Thanks for putting up with the long hours and late nights spent trying to get this book finished. You graciously ignored the threads and fabric scraps on the carpet, the pins in the cushions, and the piles of materials. Also, thanks for making me dinner—I never knew soup from a can could be so tasty!

Introduction

I have spent a lifetime designing, stitching, and collecting linens—both new and old. Following such a path was not a decision or a choice, but rather an subconscious driving force. Beautifully embroidered linens seem to be drawn to me as much as I am to them. They have a unique way of finding me and following me home wrapped-up in sheets of snowy-white tissue.

This love for embroidered linens began at a very early age. As soon as I was able to handle a needle, I was taught to sew. My mother, grandmothers, great-grandmother, and spinster aunts all made certain I was taught the necessary, ladylike skills of fine needlework.

Such was the tradition in our Spanish family, and I can still remember the day my mother gave me my very first sewing box. I was six years old, and it was nothing more than a small metal candy tin filled with a few half-empty spools of silk thread, a few needles, a thimble, and some scraps of linen upon which I was expected to practice my new skills. I was so thrilled to have my own stuff—my own little "workbasket." I was hooked!

But I wasn't content just to make embroidered linens; I also wanted to hoard them. My linen collection didn't officially begin until I was fifteen. My mother had tucked a few things away for me through the years—an embroidered bedspread made by my great-grandmother and some of the finely worked table linens made by those same highly-skilled spinster aunts—but that was the birthday I acquired my "hope chest," and it had to be filled.

The instant my paternal grandparents delivered the hope chest, I began to fill it. The first item placed tenderly in the bottom of the cedar-lined box was an heirloom set of embroidered wedding sheets from the early 1800s. These were embroidered in the old country (Spain), had once belonged to my great-great-grandmother, and had been handed down from daughter to daughter for generations. These are my most favorite treasure.

The sheets were followed by the embroidered bedspread and table linens. And with each successive birthday, more linens found their way into the chest: pillowcases, tea towels, tablecloths, doilies, and other treasures. Each year, I added more until the poor chest was ready to burst at the seams.

By the time I married, I had over 150 pieces of embroidered linens. That number has since grown—but I don't dare give the numbers, for fear that my husband will explode—I can't seem to control the urge to collect linens. But, bear in mind that I use these linens. I'm not content to let them sit in a cupboard! They are rotated often and enjoyed daily.

With this book in hand, I hope you will do the same with your treasures!

CHAPTER 1

The Well-Equipped Workbasket

Selecting Supplies for Embroidery

Fine hand embroidery has always been a popular pastime and is once again gaining momentum, and beautifully embroidered linens are once again becoming all the rage. The craze for the "shabby chic" and the "European" look has certainly helped them regain their popularity, but I think there's more to it than a simple decorating fad. People are actually *rediscovering* the joys of needlework.

New fabrics available for needlework are easy to care for and often do not require much ironing—just a light swipe with the iron and they look like new. Today's threads, unlike some of those from the past, are colorfast and durable. This means you can create great-looking linens that are machine washable, in colors that will coordinate with the décor of your own home, without the worry of the colors running during laundering or fading quickly.

To create those terrific heirlooms, you'll need to stock a few basic supplies. Here, you'll find descriptions of the various fabrics and threads used in embroidery, recommended substitutions, and the proper equipment for your workbasket.

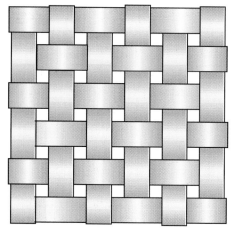

An even-weave fabric.

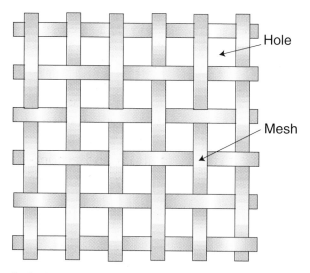

Hole

Mesh

A single-thread canvas—note the hole and mesh areas.

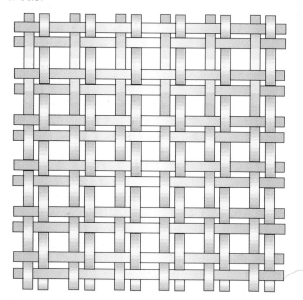

A double-thread canvas.

Selecting Fabrics for Embroidery and Needlework

Most of the projects in this book are stitched on even-weave fabrics or canvas. Even-weave means the fabric contains the same number of warp (lengthwise) and weft (crosswise) threads.

Even-weave fabrics suitable for embroidery can be made from cotton, linen, wool or blends. Some other alternatives include hemp and silk. Always use fabrics made from natural fibers because your needle will glide right through them with little or no resistance. Avoid fabrics that contain polyester because it tends to be more difficult to get a needle through because of "drag." The only exception to this rule being rayon-blend fabrics (either silk/rayon or cotton/rayon blends) because Rayon is finished in a way that makes it easy to stitch.

While most of the project materials list a specific fabric, you can change the fabric easily if it happens to be a surface-embroidered project. Projects made using counted thread techniques will require a bit of thought and/or math before changing fabrics.

Be sure to pre-wash all fabrics (except needlepoint canvas) before cutting and stitching the projects. This will prevent laundry shrinkage in the finished project, preventing a lot of heartache!

Fabrics for Surface Embroidery: Fabrics suitable for the surface embroidered projects in this book include common-weave fabrics (tightly-woven even-weave fabrics that are readily available) such as Hardanger cloth, broadcloth, chambray, oxford cloth, or other fabrics referred to as "shirting."

For surface-embroidered projects, select fabrics with higher thread counts. This allows for a tighter weave and more support for the stitches. If you choose a fabric with a low thread count (28 stitches per inch or less), the stitches don't have much of a surface to cling to and tend to look a little bit off-kilter when finished.

Fabrics for Counted-Thread Techniques: Fabrics for counted-thread embroidery, such as cross-stitch or needlepoint, include lower thread-count even-weaves, Aida cloth, needlepoint canvas, perforated paper and plastic canvas (the latter two are not fabrics at all, but are fun to stitch), and burlap. These fabrics allow you to count the threads easily.

The reason lower thread-count fabrics are suitable for this type of embroidery is because you will be stitching over a specific number of threads. For instance, if you are working cross-stitch over 2 threads of fabric and you are using fabric with a very high thread count (say, 32 for example), your cross-stitches will be minuscule and difficult to stitch at only 16 stitches per inch. Using a higher thread-count, such as 20, will result in larger cross-stitches that are easier to work at 10 stitches per inch.

Aida cloth is made especially for counted-thread embroidery and is easily distinguishable by its weave. The fabric is made in such a way that little squares of fabric are visible on the surface, indicating exactly where to stitch. One square of Aida equals one cross-stitch.

Canvas for needlepoint comes in a few varieties: tapestry, Penelope, mono and interlock, to name just a few. Mono is a single-thread canvas, while tapestry and Penelope are double-thread canvases. Canvas count is listed either by mesh size or holes-per-inch, depending on manufacturer and country of origin.

To keep things simple, all of the needlepoint projects in this book use interlock canvas, which is made by interlocking the threads of the canvas so they won't shift during the embroidery process. Interlock is available in a wide range of thread counts, but here we're stitching on 12-count canvas because it is easy to stitch and accommodates standard tapestry wool easily.

Threads for Embroidery and Needlepoint

Projects in this book are made from Anchor and DMC floss, thread, and yarns. Both brands are readily available in your local craft or needlework shop and are virtually interchangeable.

Six-strand embroidery floss is the most common thread used in embroidery. As its name implies, it is made from six strands of thread grouped together to form a hand or skein of floss. To use six-strand floss, separate the strands by cutting a length of floss no longer than your arm (18 to 22 inches), and pulling apart the strands. If you need to use 2 strands of floss in a project, you will separate the length of floss into 3 groups having 2 strands each. If you are to use 3 strands of floss, separate the length of floss into 2 groups having 3 strands each.

> ## 𝒩 Cheryl's tip:
> The rule to keep in mind with counted-thread fabrics: the higher the thread count, the smaller and tighter the stitch.

Quick-Reference Thread Conversion Chart

Use this guide to make thread substitutions for products available in your area. Each manufacturer uses a different numbering system for their colors. For instance, if a project uses Anchor floss and your local stores stock DMC floss, use the chart to find the corresponding color number.

Anchor	DMC	Color Name	Anchor	DMC	Color Name	Anchor	DMC	Color Name
9	352	Salmon Medium Light	243	988	Grass Green Medium	972	3803	Wineberry Dark
19	304	Burgundy Medium	253	772	Parrot Green Very Light	977	334	Sea Blue Medium
20	815	Burgundy Medium Dark				1002	976	Antique Gold Light
25	3716	Carnation Light	262	3363	Loden Green Medium	1016	3727	Antique Mauve Light
36	3326	Blossom Pink Light	265	3348	Avocado Light	1018	3726	Antique Mauve Dark
42	3284	Carmine Rose Medium	267	470	Avocado Medium			
46	666	Crimson Red	275	746	Citrus Ultra Light	1022 Light	760	Peony Medium
62	603	Magenta Medium	288 Light	445	Canary Yellow	1025	347	Peony Medium Dark
78	3803	Antique Rose Dark				1027	3722	Rose Wine Medium Dark
86	3608	Orchid Medium Light	289	307	Canary Yellow Medium Light	1028	3685	Raspberry Medium Dark
108	210	Lavender Light	290	972	Canary Yellow Medium	1035	930	Antique Blue Dark
109	209	Lavender MediumLight	291 Dark	444	Canary Yellow	1038	519	Glacier Blue Medium
111	208	Lavender Medium Dark	302	743	Citrus Medium Light	1039	518	Glacier Blue Medium Dark
128	775	Cobalt Blue Light	305	726	Topaz Light	1070	993	Jade Light
130	809	Cobalt Blue Medium Light	307	783	Topaz Medium	1076	991	Jade
			311	3855	Tangerine Very Light	1206	115	Variegated Red
131	798	Cobalt Blue Medium	339	920	Terra Cotta Medium	8022	7474	Dark Gold*
132	797	Cobalt Blue Medium Dark	363	436	Nutmeg Medium	8042	7484	Medium Gold*
145	3755	Delft Blue Light	380	5478	Fudge	8114	7431	Light Yellow*
146	322	Delft Blue	392	642	Linen Medium	8120	7050	Dark Yellow*
150	336	Delft Blue Dark	683	6880	Turf Green	8220	7218	Deep Maroon*
164	3842	Sapphire Dark	843	3053	Fern Green	8254	7762	Light Peach*
206	564	Spruce Light	846	3051	Fern Green Dark	8258	7012	Dark Peach*
214	368	Juniper Light	874	834	Saffron Medium	8396	7760	Light Pink*
215	6017	Juniper Medium Light	875	3817	Pine Light	8402	7207	Dark Pink*
			876	3816	Pine	8524	7253	Light Lilac*
216	367	Juniper Medium	877	3815	Pine Medium	8528	7257	Dark Lilac*
217	367	Juniper Medium Dark	878	501	Pine Medium Dark	8624	7035	Light Blue*
			890	436	Brass Light	8630	7317	Medium Blue*
218	319	Juniper Dark	894	224	Rose Wine Medium Light	9002	7369	Light Green*
228	700	Emerald Medium Dark	907	783	Saffron Dark	9006	7320	Medium Grass Green
229	700	Emerald Dark	970	3726	Wineberry Medium Dark	9022	7890	Dark Green*

*Tapestry Wool Colors

Pearl cotton is used in several of the surface-embroidery projects. It is a single-strand yarn of high-luster cotton in a variety of sizes, including #3, #5, #8 and #12. A higher number indicates a finer thread. In this book the size used is #8, which is equivalent to about 3 strands of 6-strand floss, if you should prefer to substitute floss in a project.

Tapestry wool is used for all of the needlepoint projects. This is a 100% wool, fine-gauge 4-ply yarn. The 4-plies can be separated as for six-strand floss, but here you'll use the yarn as-is, straight from the skein without separating the plies. Tapestry yarn is also available in a less-expensive acrylic version, but the wool is so much nicer to work with and the finished results are much better, as acrylic tends to have a luster that is undesirable in needlepoint.

Cheryl's tip:

For best results, be sure to fully separate the strands of floss and re-group them. This will make for tidier stitching and will also help prevent tangling.

Trims and Things

Trims, such as piping, lace, ribbons and such, are used to finish off a project, but are always optional. When purchasing trims, always buy the best you can afford. After spending hour after hour creating your special project, don't ruin it by adding bargain-basement lace!

Also, when purchasing trims for your project, pay close attention to the seam allowance (the area of the trim that will be enclosed in the stitching). This is especially true with piping. These seam allowances can range in size from 1/4 inch to more than 1/2 inch.

If your project uses 1/4-inch seam allowances but the trim uses 1/2 inch, you'll have to adjust the seam allowances on the project by adding the necessary 1/4 inch along all sides to accommodate the larger seam allowance. The same is true in reverse, but you'll be removing the 1/4 inch of extra seam allowance on all sides of the project.

A good rule of thumb is the wider the seam allowance, the chunkier the trim. Tips for stitching trims in place can be found in Chapter 4.

Cheryl's tip:

Be sure to pre-wash all trims before using to prevent shrinkage in your finished project.

The Embroiderer's Equipment

Only a few basic materials, in addition to fabric and thread, are necessary for embroidery. Most of them will fit tidily into a tote bag or workbasket. Other items, such as floor-standing scroll frames, are larger or more cumbersome and will need to be used at home.

Hoops, Scroll Frames, Stretcher Bars and Stands

All embroidery should be placed in a hoop or frame while being worked. These devices keep the fabric taut, helping to avoid puckering and distortion as you stitch. Many of these have optional floor stands available for working larger pieces.

Embroidery hoops are a familiar piece of equipment to most people. They are used for surface embroidery or cross-stitch projects, and are available in a range of sizes. They can be circular or oval in shape, and are made from wood, plastic, or metal. The embroidery fabric is placed between the two pieces of the hoop, and the outer hoop is then tightened around the inner hoop and fabric by means of a screw or spring.

Use smaller hoops for small projects, and bigger hoops for larger ones. The oval hoops are helpful when stitching a border area, such as on pillowcases, sheets and tablecloths, because more of the workable area is displayed at one time.

Scroll frames are used for needlepoint or cross-stitch and may or may not come equipped with a stand that sits on a table or on the floor. Others come equipped with a table clamp or a stand that you sit on while working the embroidery. Selecting the type of stand is a matter of personal preference. I prefer to use a frame on a stand so I can keep both hands free to work, rather than holding the frame in one hand and embroidering with the other.

To use a scroll frame, the fabric is attached to the upper and lower roll bars. To move from one fabric area to another, roll the bars in the direction necessary to get to the right spot.

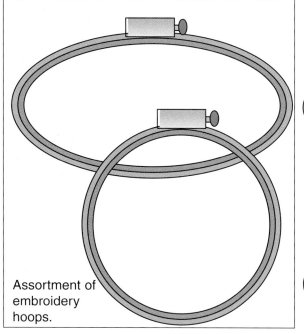

Assortment of embroidery hoops.

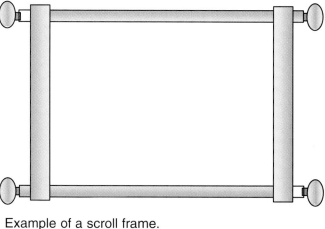

Example of a scroll frame.

Stretcher bars are generally used for needlepoint, tapestry and some cross stitch, and are made from dovetailed lengths of wood that are connected together to form a square or rectangle. The fabric or canvas is then stapled or attached to the frame with thumbtacks to prepare it for embroidery. The bars are sold in sets of 2 so you can easily assemble a frame that is just right for the project.

Select frame pieces that are at least 4 inches larger than the project, and cut the project fabric slightly larger than the frame. The reason for this is once the project is finished and removed from the frame, you'll want to trim away the fabric areas that were secured with the staples, and cut the fabric to the proper size.

Universal *stands* are available to accommodate your hoop, frames, or stretcher bars if your model did not come already equipped with one. These can be either floor or table-standing models. Both feature a clamp to hold your item in place securely as you stitch, leaving your hands free.

Selecting the Right Needle

Needles can be short or long, have large eyes (holes) or small ones, or be sharp or blunt and rounded at the end. Selection is based both on the type of embroidery you are doing, and the thickness of the thread or yarn you are using.

Names for the needles include tapestry, sharps, crewel and chenille—and sometimes are simply labeled "embroidery" or "cross-stitch" needles. The larger the size number is on the package, the sharper and shorter the needle will be!

Always select a needle with an eye that will easily accommodate your thread, without having the thread too loose. You should be able to thread the needle easily, but not leave a gaping hole behind as you stitch.

The types of needles normally used for *surface embroidery* are sharp, so they can easily penetrate the surface of the fabric. Recommended needles and sizes are sharps or crewel needles in sizes 5 through 10.

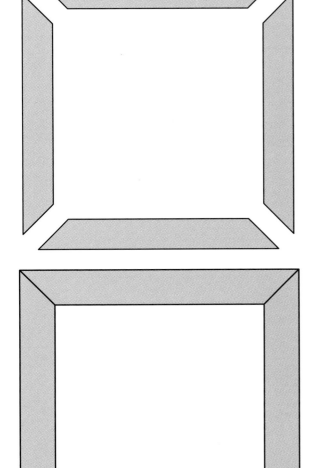

Stretcher bars both before and after assembly.

Needles used for *counted cross-stitch* and *needlepoint* are blunt-tipped and are usually referred to as tapestry or cross stitch needles (depending on the size). The blunt tip allows the needle to glide *between* the threads of the fabric or canvas, rather than pierce them. This helps keep the stitching neat and helps to avoid catching the base fabric in the stitch (which can ruin the base fabric or cause distortion). Good needle sizes for cross-stitch are 5 through 26, and sizes 18 through 22 for needlepoint.

An assortment of standard sewing needles (sharps) is also handy to keep on hand in your workbasket for hemming, basting, or assembling projects.

Cheryl's tip:

To thread a needle when using a bulky thread, wrap the end of the yarn around the eye and pinch it tightly between the thumb and forefinger, making a crease on the fold where the thread doubles back on itself. While pinching, slide the yarn up over the eye and off the needle—still pinching. Now, push the creased area through the eye of the needle. It takes some practice, but works much better than licking the ends of the yarn and trying to push them through! If you still have difficulty threading your needle, use a needle-threader. They're available in different sizes for different types of yarns and threads.

Necessary Notions

There are only a few more items you'll need to include in your workbasket:

A retractable tape measure (standard measuring tapes get tangled easily).

Water-soluble marking pencils or tailor's chalk for marking designs on fabric—be sure to test them to be sure they do indeed wash completely out of the fabric before marking anything (no No. 2 pencils!).

Small embroidery scissors for cutting threads.

Larger all-purpose scissors for cutting fabric and canvas.

Needle threaders (optional).

A needle case to keep your needles secure and to avoid loss or unnecessary surprises when reaching into the bag or basket.

Thimbles to protect your pushing finger when using sharp needles.

T-pins for blocking finishing projects.

Regular pins for other uses.

A free-standing or hand-held magnifier, or reading glasses if needed.

Masking tape for edge-finishing canvas.

Seam sealant for edge-finishing fabrics.

All-purpose thread for edge-finishing. fabrics.

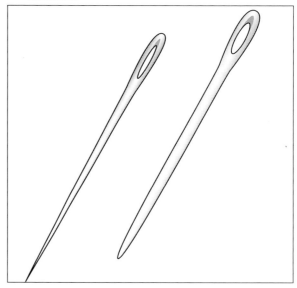

Sharp and blunt-tipped needles.

CHAPTER 2

Preparing

for

Embroidery

Preparing the Fabric

If there's one thing I can't stress too frequently, it's the importance of preparing your fabric properly. This includes prewashing and edge finishing. Both are very important and should not be skipped unless you're a glutton for punishment! Preshrinking and the removal of coatings are essential to a well-made finished project, and no one likes the hassle of having their embroidery thread, or yarn, catching and fraying as they stitch.

Prewashing Fabrics and Supplies

All fabrics and trims, if machine washable, should be prewashed, dried and pressed before starting a project. This will not only preshrink the fabrics and trims, but also removes any coatings that have been applied during the manufacturing process. Sometimes these coatings can cause needle drag, making the project more difficult to stitch. Prewashing also removes excess dye and lint.

Fabrics that are not machine-washable, such as needlepoint canvas, can be used as-is. Wool fabrics should be dry-cleaned before use.

Trims that are made from cotton or rayon should also be prewashed before use. This includes lace, piping or insertions.

Edge-Finishing Basics

Before taking a single stitch, you will need to edge-finish your fabric or canvas. Edge-finishing will prevent fraying around the edges of the fabric, and will also guard against having the embroidery thread or yarn "catch" on the stiff fibers that poke out from the edges of needlepoint canvas. There are several ways to edge-finish your embroidery fabrics.

For fabrics such as even-weaves or Aida cloth, you can edge-finish them several ways. First, you can apply a liquid seam-sealant around the edges of the fabric. When dry, the sealant acts as glue to hold the fibers together.

A second alternative is to machine-stitch around the raw edges of the fabric with zigzag stitching, using all-purpose thread.

For ground fabrics such as needlepoint canvas, edge-finish them by applying a length of 2-inch wide masking tape around the edges of the canvas. This is the preferred method of most needlepoint stitchers. The tape will be cut away later, along with the excess canvas. You can also fold under the edges and whipstitch them in place, but it is more time consuming and doesn't prevent the embroidery thread or yarn from "catching" as well as masking tape.

To help you locate projects suitable to your level of skill, all instructions in this book feature a rating system based on needles. There are one-, two- or three-needle ratings assigned to each project.

While all of the projects in this book are easy, some are designed with the rank beginner in mind. These projects have been assigned a one-needle rating.

Other projects require a few basic sewing skills and have been given a two-needle rating.

There are only a handful of three-needle rated projects. These either feature a new stitch to learn, or are larger projects taking more time to complete.

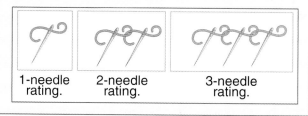

1-needle rating.   2-needle rating.   3-needle rating.

Applying seam sealant to the fabric edges.

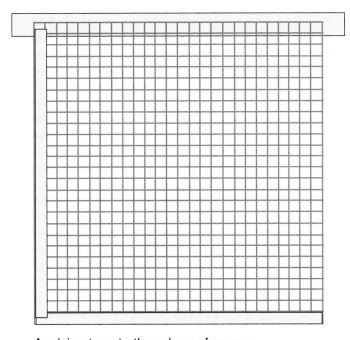

Applying tape to the edges of canvas.

Zigzag around the edges of the fabric.

Transferring the Patterns to Fabric

Transferring the embroidery patterns to the fabric need not be a daunting task. If you follow a few basic guidelines and use a water-soluble marking pencil, you'll have no problem removing the lines from the fabric later.

First and foremost, be sure to test the marking pencil on a scrap of fabric to be certain it will wash out. To test the pencil, mark a few lines on your prewashed fabric scrap. Press it with a hot iron and then wash it in room-temperature water with a bit of mild soap. If the marks came out in the wash, the pencil is fine and dandy to use. If it did not come out, try a different brand.

Never use an ordinary No. 2 pencil because it often becomes permanent. Also, don't use pencils marked "transfer pencils" because these are meant for transferring patterns using a hot iron and they are permanent!

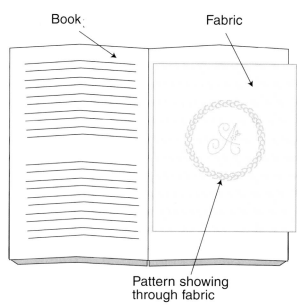

Book   Fabric

Pattern showing through fabric

Tracing a pattern directly onto fabric.

Tracing the Patterns to Fabric

To trace an embroidery design onto a light-colored fabric, center the fabric directly over the pattern and trace. If you can't see the pattern through the fabric use a light source, such as a window or light box, to shine light through the pattern and fabric, making it easier to see.

For darker fabrics, use a light source, or light-colored transfer or carbon paper (yellow, white or light blue work best). Be sure you are using dressmaker's transfer paper and that it will wash out of the fabric (test this like you would a pencil—see previous paragraphs). To use the transfer paper or dressmaker's carbon, position the carbon colored-side-down on the fabric and the pattern right side up on the carbon. Trace using a blunt pen or pencil (a dead ballpoint pen is ideal).

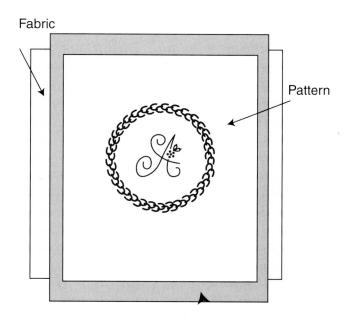

Fabric

Pattern

Carbon paper

Transferring a pattern using carbon.

Chapter 3

Embroidery

Stitch

Details

Counted Thread Stitches

There are only three stitches in this book that fall into the counted thread category, but these three stitches are the most important, and often form the basis for other stitches. These three stitches are counted cross-stitch, tent-stitch and Scotch-stitch.

Counted-thread stitches are worked over a specified number of threads, squares or holes in fabric or canvas—hence their name—and they are some of the easiest to master. Below are the three basic stitches you will need to learn to make some of the projects featured in Chapter 5.

Counted Cross-Stitch

This stitch is worked either over a specified number of stitches, squares (such as the squares formed by the weave of Aida fabric) or holes in canvas or perforated paper. To work a row of cross-stitches, work the stitches that slant to the right first, followed by those that slant to the left. The same is true of working a single cross-stitch.

To ensure a neatly-stitched final product, be sure to have all of the stitches slanting in the same direction—this will also help keep the backside of the work tidy.

Tent-Stitch

The tent-stitch—also known as the Continental-stitch—is the most common needlepoint stitch you will ever encounter. It is worked over the intersections on needlepoint canvas. It's basically a half cross-stitch, worked from right to left.

Scotch-Stitch

This is a filling stitch used in two of the needlepoint projects in Chapter 5. It is made from basic tent stitches of differing lengths, arranged in a square pattern. The numbered figure in the lower right corner shows the order of stitching: the needle comes up at 1 and down at 2, up at 3 and down at 4, up at 5 and down at 6, and so on.

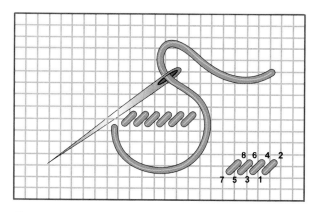

Example of tent-stitch.

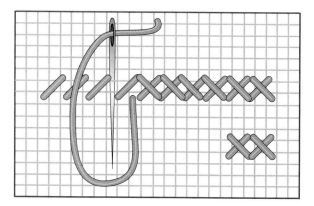

Example of cross-stitch.

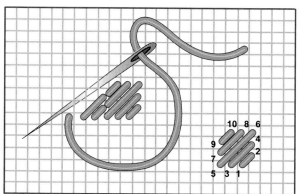

Example of scotch-stitch.

Free-Style Surface Stitches

Free-style surface stitches are some of the easiest stitches to learn, and are the ones that are most frequently used to create linens with an old-world charm.

While this family of stitches has many names, I prefer to use this term to describe those stitches that sit on top of the fabric—hence the term 'surface' or those that do not require a counted ground. For example, when stitching a project in counted cross-stitch or needlepoint, the stitches merge with the base fabric, and often form the groundwork of the design.

But free-style surface stitches are free flowing and seem to float on the surface of the fabric. They do not merge with the ground fabric—they stand on their own.

The following examples and illustrations describe each stitch used in this book.

Running-Stitch

This is probably the very first stitch anyone ever learns. It's a basic! The needle simply moves in and out of the fabric at evenly-spaced intervals, forming a dashed line of thread.

Backstitch

Backstitch is worked by taking a stitch backwards along a line. It's a simple stitch that produces a very thin outline. To work this stitch, the needle comes up through the fabric at 1, down at 2, and up again at 3. In this book it is used often to stitch delicate lines and tendrils.

Stem- and Outline-Stitch

These two stitches are worked almost identically to each other. The only difference between them is the width of the finished stitch.

In outline-stitch (lower left) the needle pierces the fabric along the marked line—up at 1, down at 2, up at 3. But, the stitching is worked entirely along the marked line, giving a thin appearance, which is great for outlining or for thin stems.

In stem-stitch (lower right), the needle pierces the fabric slightly above and below the marked line. This makes a thicker line of stitching suitable for fatter stems and chunky outlines.

Chain-Stitch

This stitch, when worked along a line, resembles a linked chain. It makes a terrific filling stitch or outline stitch. It takes a bit of time to master, so be sure to practice on scrap fabric first. The trick to a perfect chain stitch is not to pull the loops of thread too tightly. To work the stitch, lift up a short length of fabric and loop the thread around the underside of the needle. Pull the needle through the loop. To make a continuous line of chains, re-insert the needle inside the last loop formed to begin the next loop.

Lazy-Daisy Stitch

This stitch belongs to the chain-stitch family. The loops are formed in the same way as the links in chain stitch, by looping the thread under the needle. But, instead of making a line of stitches, the loops are formed in a circular shape, resembling a daisy.

Single or Detached Chain

Also from the chain stitch family, the single chain is formed from a single loop. It's used mainly for small leaves or flower buds. It's made in the same manner as the lazy-daisy stitch, but using only one unit at a time.

French Knots

This is one of the most-feared stitches, but is actually one of the easiest and most versatile you could have in your repertoire! It's formed by wrapping the thread around the needle twice, and re-inserting the needle close to the original hole.

Practice the stitch on some scrap fabric first—the important thing to keep in mind when making this stitch is to watch your tension. Do not wrap the thread too tightly around the needle, or you will find yourself pulling the knot to the backside of the fabric, rather than leaving it on the front where you need it. The thread should not be too loose, either. Practice makes perfect.

Cross-Stitch

Working cross-stitch as an embroidery fabric is usually done on pre-stamped fabrics, such as linens and pillowcases. It's worked in the same manner as counted cross-stitch, but you follow the printed lines on the fabric, rather than counting threads.

Herringbone-Stitch

Herringbone-stitch is similar to a cross-stitch, but all the crosses are connected by "legs." It really does not need much explanation, because it's a very simple stitch, worked along 2 lines on the fabric—the upper and lower lines. Keep the spacing even for best results.

Fern-Stitch

This nifty accent stitch is worked by making a group of three backstitches, having their bottoms in the same spot. They can be worked individually or in a line. You'll use this stitch in the Redwork Coverlet in Chapter 5.

Seed-Stitch

This is a filling stitch. It is worked by taking up small, random stitches inside a larger area (which is often outlined in stem-, backstitch or outline-stitch).

Satin-Stitch

This stitch is worked by filling an area with long, flat stitches, spaced closely together. This gives the area to be filled a "satiny" appearance and gives the stitch its name. It's a real floss-hog, so be sure to have plenty on hand when working this stitch.

If you want to have the cross-stitch area raised up a bit, fill the area with seed-stitch before working the satin-stitch.

Four-sided Stitch

This stitch is mainly used as an outline stitch for large areas, such as on the Country Rose Dresser Runner in Chapter 5. It's made from a combination of straight-stitch and backstitch to form small, joined squares. Don't pull the thread too tightly when working this stitch.

Examples of Free-Style Surface Stitches

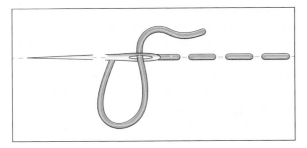

Running-stitch.

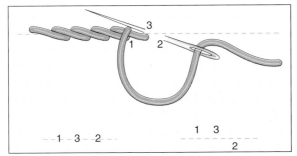

Stem-stitch.

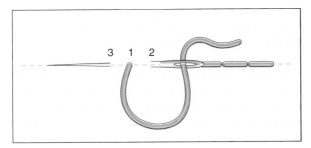

Backstitch.

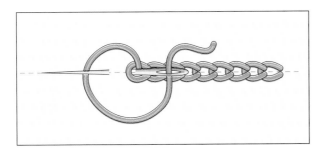

Chain-stitch.

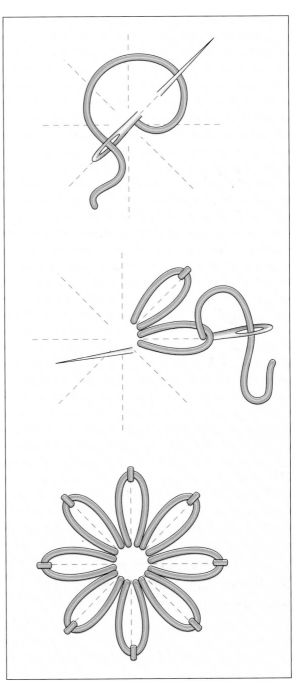

Lazy-daisy stitch.

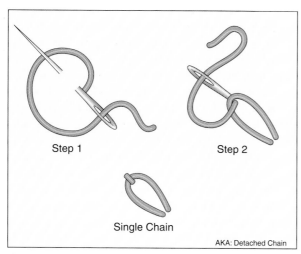

Step 1   Step 2

Single Chain

AKA: Detached Chain

Single chain.

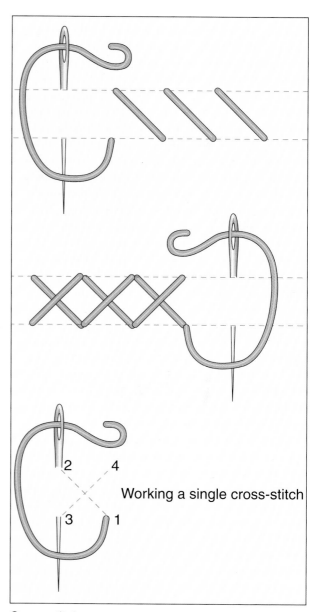

Working a single cross-stitch

Cross-stitch.

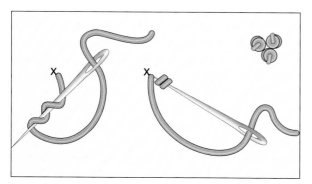

French knot.

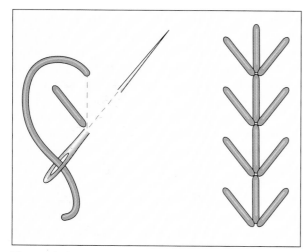

Fern-stitch.

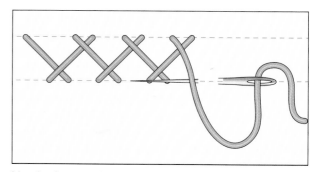

Herringbone stitch.

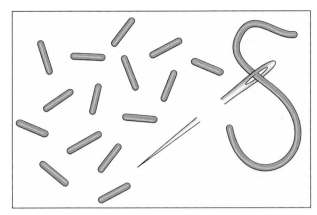

Seed-stitch.

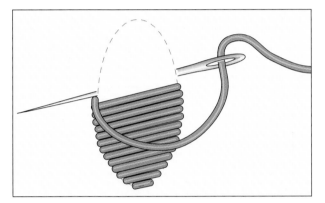

Satin-stitch.

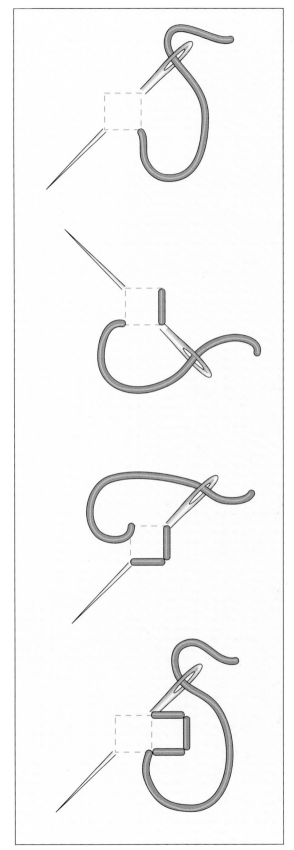

Four-sided stitch.

CHAPTER 4

The Finishing Touches

Pressing and Blocking

Every finished project must be cleaned and pressed or blocked. Oils from your hands (and other odd things) find their way onto your project as you stitch and need to be removed before you finish or use them.

Pressing Fabric-Based Projects

To clean an embroidered fabric piece, fill a basin with room-temperature water and a mild liquid detergent. Gently swish the item in the soapy water for a few seconds. Follow with several rinses in room-temperature water.

Remove the excess water from the project by rolling it in a nice, fluffy bath towel. Do not wrinkle or wring the fabric to remove the excess water because this will stretch—and potentially damage—the fibers in both the fabric and the stitching. Treat your projects with tender loving care!

Once the excess water has been removed and is almost dry, press fabric-based pieces with an iron set to the type of fabric it is made from—usually cotton or linen. To press properly, lift the iron before you move to the next spot. Pressing should always be done in an up-and-down motion.

The reason for the up-and-down pressing motion is so you won't stretch the fabric as it is pressed, which often leaves creases. Once the fabric is completely dry, however, ironing with a sliding motion is perfectly acceptable and helps to remove any iron shadows left from the pressing motion.

①

Needlework face down

Roll the project in a towel to remove excess water.

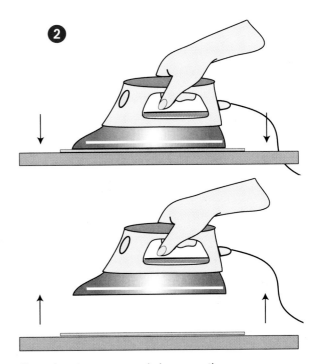

②

Pressing is an up-and-down motion.

③

Ironing is done with a sliding motion.

Blocking a Needlepoint Project

To block (straighten-out) a needlepoint piece, dampen the project with room-temperature water using a squirt bottle. (Note: if the piece of needlepoint is heavily soiled, have it dry-cleaned before blocking.)

Attach the project to a blocking board, which can be purchased at fabric and crafts stores. A blocking board is a lightweight piece of wood, padded and covered with a fabric marked with a grid of one-inch squares. Using T-pins, fasten the project to the board, straightening it out as you pull it into shape, using the grid lines as a guide. The "Tabriz" needlepoint pillow from Chapter 5 is shown as an example.

When the project is completely dry (give it at least a couple days), remove the project from the blocking board and finish it into whatever it is you are making. Make certain the project is completely dry before removing it from the board, or it will find a way to re-distort itself again.

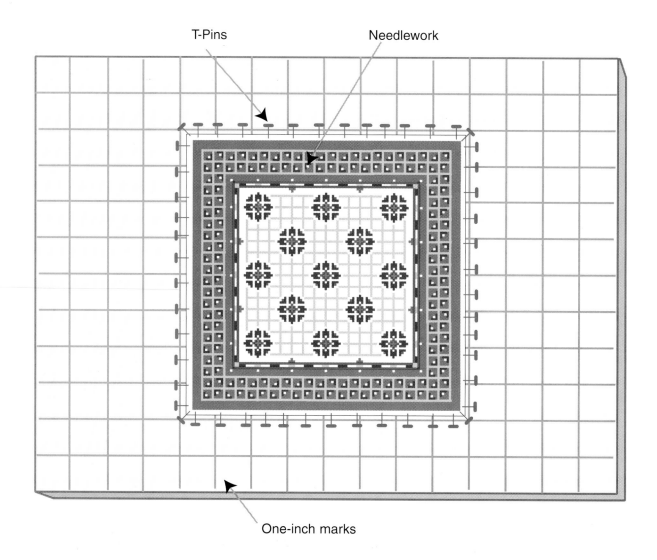

T-Pins

Needlework

One-inch marks

Pin the project to the blocking board with T-pins.

Finishing a Project

Attaching Piping or Trims to a Project

Stitching piping, laces, or trims to a project is relatively simple. After trimming the fabric or canvas down to the needed size (with seam allowances), lay the project face-up, having the right side facing you. The example here shows piping being attached to a pillow front.

Position the trim so that the seam allowance edge of the trim is even with the raw edges of the project. The decorative part of the trim—or as shown here, the rounded edge of the piping—lies towards the inside area.

Stitch the piping in place by hand, or by machine using a zipper foot, along the seam allowance. The stitching should be done as close to the rounded edge of the piping as possible, without intruding into it. Make a small clip into the seam allowance of the piping at the corners to turn them. This will allow the piping to lie flat, rather than curl when the project is turned right-side out.

Overlap the ends of the piping along the bottom edge to conceal them. Then, trim them even with the raw edges of the pillow front.

Adding Mitered-Borders to a Pillow

Pillows can be easily made from smaller-sized projects by adding matching borders to them. An example is the "Tabriz" pillow found in Chapter 5.

To make a mitered border, the four border strips are cut slightly longer than the finished size of the pillow (for instance, if you want to make a 14-inch pillow, they are cut to16 inches in length). Fold each strip in half and press to mark the centers of the strips (indicated by the line on the accompanying illustration).

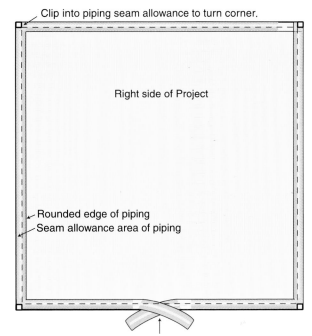

Clip into piping seam allowance to turn corner.

Right side of Project

Rounded edge of piping
Seam allowance area of piping

Overlap ends of piping along bottom edge and trim them off.

Attaching piping to a pillow front.

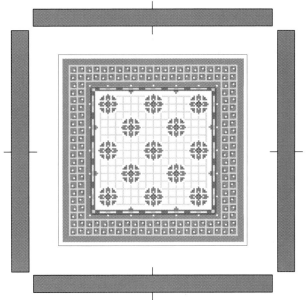

Locating the centers of the border strips.

Step 1

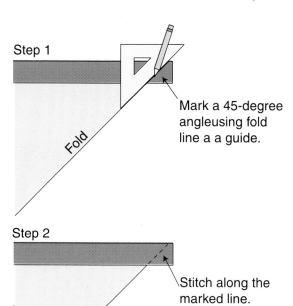

Mark a 45-degree angleusing fold line a a guide.

Step 2

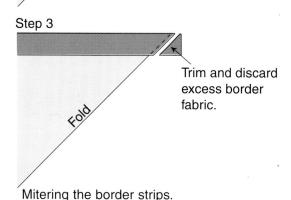

Stitch along the marked line.

Step 3

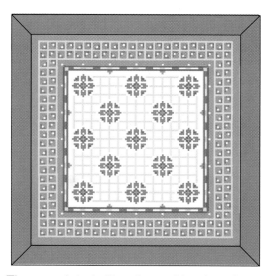

Trim and discard excess border fabric.

Mitering the border strips.

The completed pillow front with mitered corners.

Pin each strip to the center of each side of the pillow front, having the raw edges of one long edge of each strip even with the raw edge of the pillow seam allowances, and their right sides together. Stitch the borders to the pillow front.

Fold the pillow front diagonally, having the right-sides facing. Using a 45-degree triangle and a water-soluble marking pencil, mark a line from the crease of the pillow front to the edges of the border strips (step 1).

Align the two border strips that came together during the diagonal fold neatly. Stitch along the marked line (step 2).

Trim the excess border strip 1/2 inch from the stitching line and discard the excess border fabric (step 3). Repeat for all 4 sides of the pillow front and press the mitered seam allowances open. Add piping or trims, or stitch into a pillow covering.

Stitching a Pillow Covering

To stitch the project into a pillow covering, first add the trim, piping, or lace to the edges of the project (see the beginning of this chapter). Add borders if desired.

Clip corners close to but not through stitching.

Wrong side of pillow cover

Leave open for turning.

Stitching a pillow cover.

Lay the completed pillow front on the backing fabric, having their right-sides together. Stitch around the edges of the pillow (using the seam allowance size specified in the instructions), leaving an opening along the bottom edge. This will be the turning and stuffing opening.

Clip the corners of the pillow cover close to but not through the stitching, and discard the little fabric triangles. Clipping the corners in this manner will allow for nice, sharp edges when the pillow covering is turned right side out, avoiding those ugly rounded corners. It will also prevent the pillow cover from curling inwards.

After clipping the corners, turn the pillow cover right side out through the opening at the bottom. Insert the pillow form and hand-stitch the opening closed to complete the project.

Hemming a Project

Anything made from fabric will need to be hemmed or otherwise finished to keep the edges of the fabric from unraveling during use. Select all-purpose thread in a color to match the fabric and proceed with any of the following hemming techniques. They can be stitched by hand or machine.

Single-fold Hem: A single-fold hem is used if you will be attaching lace to a project (such as on a tablecloth) and you don't want the bulk of a traditional doubled-fold hem. It is the simplest of all hems.

To make a single-fold hem, turn under the edge-finished sides 1/4 to 1/2 inch. Stitch the hem in place with all-purpose thread to match the fabric.

Next you would attach your lace edging to the piece, concealing the edge-finished area under the edging.

Double-fold Hem: A double-fold hem is the traditional method of finishing a project that will not have lace or trims attached to the edges. Because this hem is folded over twice, the raw edges of the fabric are neatly concealed within the hem.

To make a double-fold hem, turn under the first fold as for the single-fold hem. Then, turn it under a second time. Stitch the hem in place using all-purpose thread to match the fabric.

Turn under the hem of edge-finished fabric to the wrong side.

wrong side

wrong side

right side

Making a single-fold hem.

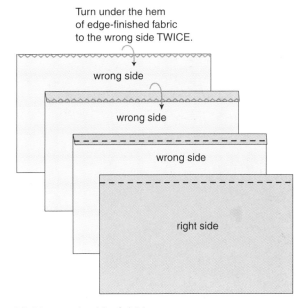

Turn under the hem of edge-finished fabric to the wrong side TWICE.

wrong side

wrong side

wrong side

right side

Making a double-fold hem.

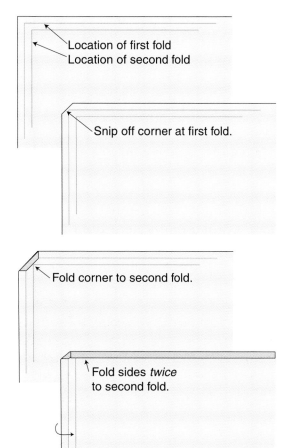

Miter-hemming a Corner: A miter-hemmed corner helps reduce the bulk associated with conjoining edges of a double-folded hem. It looks especially nice when used on napkins.

To make a mitered corner, trim off each corner to the location of the first fold. Fold this snipped edge under to the location of the second fold. Finally, turn under the remaining sides of the item twice, forming a double-fold hem.

Hemming Along a Curved Edge: Hemming a curved edge, such as on a rounded doily or tablecloth, can be tricky. The solution to the excess bulk in the hem is to gather softly along the first fold to accommodate the curve. This method can be used with both the single- and double-fold hems.

Steps one and two of a miter-hemmed corner.

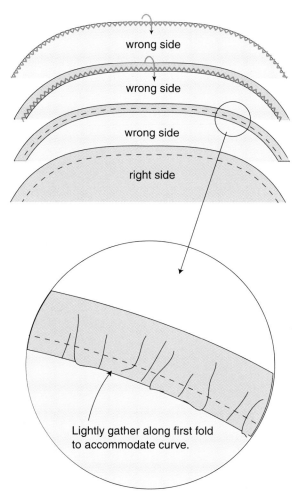

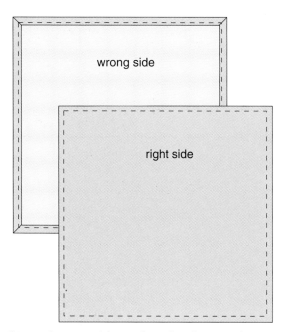

Steps three and four of a miter-hemmed corner.

Hemming a curved edge.

Hemstitching and Drawn-thread Techniques

Hemstitching and drawn-thread stitching give linens a quality, old-world feel. Although these techniques are not at all difficult to stitch, they are often shown on projects but rarely taught in most needlework books.

While there are dozens upon dozens of different hemstitch and drawn-thread stitches, we'll stick the most basic ones here—just to get you started.

Basic Hemstitch: The projects in this book requiring hemstitching will tell you to remove a crosswise thread from the fabric at a certain location. The hemstitch is then worked in the resulting gap, from left to right, using sewing thread. This stitch can be worked along any gap or along the hem (as the name implies).

Starting with your needle two crosswise threads below the gap, bring your needle up and around the designated number of lengthwise threads. In the example shown here, we're taking up a bundle of four lengthwise threads.

Next, insert your needle from behind, and bring it up again two crosswise threads below the gap. Repeat the process for the length of the gap.

To work the hemstitch along a hemmed edge, fold under the desired hem width twice and baste in place. Remove the crosswise thread from the fabric at the point where the first hem fold meets the fabric. Work the hemstitch along the resulting gap, catching all layers of the hem in the stitching.

For fabrics with a high thread-count, take up bundles of 4 threads. For those with a lower thread count (the chunkier fabrics) take 2 or 3 threads per bundle. The example here shows 4 threads per bundle. When you have finished stitching the hem, remove the basting threads.

To work a wider band of hemstitch-

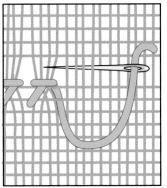 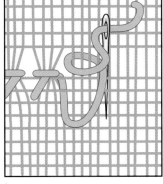

The basic hemstitch in two steps.

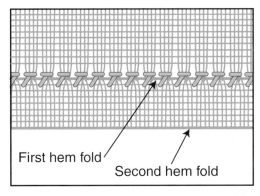

Working the hemstitch along a doubled hem.

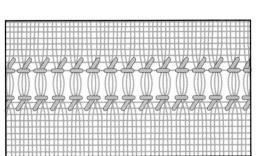

Ladder hemstitching.

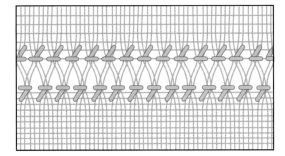

Serpentine hemstitching.

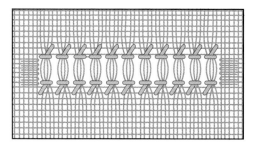

Hemstitching a small area of fabric.

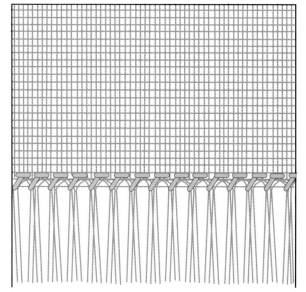

Hemstitched fringe.

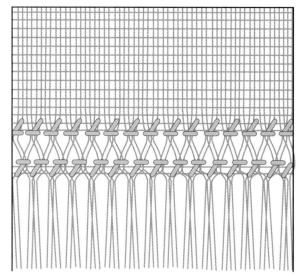

Hemstitching with fringe.

ing on fabric, remove additional crosswise threads and work the hemstitch along both sides of the gap. This is called either a double hemstitch or a ladder hemstitch.

The zigzag or serpentine hemstitch is worked in the same manner, except the bundles on the opposing sides are split, creating a nifty wave effect.

Hemstitching can also be worked along the center area of fabric. To work it in this manner, clip the crosswise threads one inch from each desired end, then weave the threads back into the fabric with a needle. After re-weaving the threads, hemstitch along the gap.

The same stitch can also be used to create a fringe along the edges of the fabric. To work a fringe, remove a crosswise thread just above the area you want fringed. Work the hemstitch along the gap. To finish, remove the remaining crosswise threads below the hemstitched area.

In Chapter 5, the "Cross-Stitch Grapes" towel and runner set features both hemstitching and fringe. To create this pattern, first fringe the edge. Next, remove the designated number of crosswise threads from the area above the fringe and work the hemstitch along the opposite gap.

The

Projects

PROJECT 1

Yellow Blossoms Embroidered Bed Linens

Although this project may look difficult, looks can be deceiving! It's actually one of the simplest projects in this book and is suitable for a beginner. The little blossoms are quick to stitch, and the results are lovely. Only four colors of embroidery floss are used in this project—two shades of green and two of yellow—making it easy to change the colors to suit your own tastes.

The project is made from a set of purchased bed sheets. Use any size you wish, but make certain they are of good quality. If you are going to put the effort and time into embroidering these sheets, you will want them to be durable. If desired, add flat lace along the edges for a pretty finishing touch.

MATERIALS NEEDED:

- Set of white sheets in the desired size
- Flat-lace trim (optional) to fit around all pillow openings and along the length of the sheet band.
- Three skeins each (for twin and double sizes) or five skeins each (for queen and king sizes) of six-strand embroidery floss in the following colors:

Anchor#	DMC#		Color Name
291	444		Canary Yellow Dark
307	783		Topaz Medium
1070	993		Jade Light
1076	991		Jade

STITCHES USED:

Stem-stitch or outline-stitch
Lazy-daisy

DIFFICULTY LEVEL:

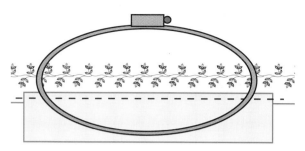

Securing the sheet edge in the hoop using a band of scrap fabric.

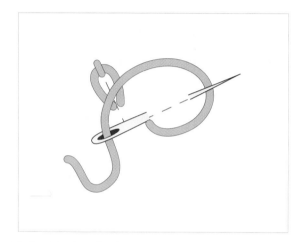

Embroidering the leaves.

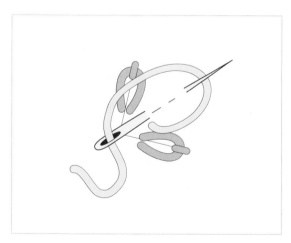

The two-tone embroidered flower.

MAKING THE PROJECT

1. Pre-wash the set of sheets and the flat lace to shrink the items and remove any coatings on the fabric. Removing the coatings allows your needle to glide through the fabric easily.

2. Using a washable pencil, trace the repeating pattern for embroidery, centering it on the bands of the pillowcases and the band on the flat top sheet. Place one of the items in an embroidery hoop.

3. Cut a length of Jade embroidery floss no longer than the length of your arm and separate the strands. Using two of the six strands in your needle, embroider along the stem lines using the stem-stitch.

4. Cut a length of the Jade Light floss and separate the strands. Using three of the six strands in your needle, embroider the leaves in the lazy-daisy stitch (single chain).

5. Cut a length of Canary Yellow floss and separate the strands. Using three of the six strands in your needle, embroider the two outer flower petals in the lazy-daisy stitch. Repeat for the inner petal using the Topaz Medium floss.

6. When you have completed all of the embroidery, hand- or machine-stitch the lace to the edges of the sheet and pillowcases, if desired.

7. Wash and press the finished linens before using.

Cheryl's tip:

If you are having difficulty keeping the sheet band tight in the embroidery hoop, attach a band of scrap fabric along the edge to help secure it. The band of fabric gives the hoop more fabric to grab and hold.

To make the band, cut a strip of fabric 8 inches wide and 18 inches long. Hand-stitch the strip to the edge of the sheet using long, running stitches (so they are easy to remove when you move the band to the next spot). Move the strip of fabric from one area to the next as you complete a section.

The full-size repeating embroidery pattern for the Yellow Blossoms Linens.

Alternate Sheet Bands

Here are two additional sheet band designs for you to embroider! A set of two would make a lovely bridal or housewarming gift.

To use the designs on the sheets, simply trace the repeating pattern along the center of the sheet band for the entire length of the band. You'll need to purchase extra floss if embroidering the design on sheets —two to three skeins of each color should suffice.

DIFFICULTY LEVEL:

MAKING THE PROJECTS:

NOTE: Separate the six-strand floss into groups of 3 strands. You will use 3 strands of the floss in your needle throughout the project.

1. Pre-wash the set of sheets and the flat lace to pre-shrink the items and remove any coatings on the fabric. Removing the coatings allows your needle to glide through the fabric easily.

2. Using a washable pencil, trace the repeating pattern for embroidery, centering it on the bands of the pillowcases. Secure the pillowcase in an embroidery hoop.

MATERIALS NEEDED FOR THE ROSEBUD DESIGN:

- Pre-purchased pillow cases
- Flat-lace trim (optional) to fit around the pillow openings One skeins each (for twin and double sizes) or five skeins each (for queen and king sizes) of 6-strand Embroidery Floss in the following colors:

Anchor#	DMC#		Color Name
876	(3816)		Pine
218	(319)		Juniper Dark
363	(436)		Nutmeg Medium
972	(3803)		Wineberry Dark

MATERIALS NEEDED FOR THE LATTICE DESIGN:

- Pre-purchased pillow cases
- Flat-lace trim (optional) to fit around the pillow openings One skeins each (for twin and double sizes) or five skeins each (for queen and king sizes) of 6-strand Embroidery Floss in the following colors:

Anchor#	DMC#		Color Name
108	(210)		Lavender Light
243	(988)		Grass Green Medium
1038	(519)		Glacier Blue Medium
1039	(518)		Glacier Blue Medium Dark
1002	(976)		Antique Gold Light

STITCHES USED:

Straight-stitch, Lazy-daisy, French knot, Stem-stitch or Outline-stitch, Satin-stitch, Back-stitch.

3. For the Rosebud design, referring to the pattern, embroider as follows: embroider the stems in stem or outline stitch using color 876 Pine. Stitch one side of the leaves in satin-stitch using color 876 Pine. Embroider the other side of the leaves using color 218 Juniper Dark in satin-stitch.

4. Embroider the flower outline and detail in outline stitch using color 972 Wineberry Dark. Embroider the center of the flowers in French knots using color 363 Nutmeg Medium. Also using Nutmeg Medium, embroider the lower petals in lazy-daisy stitch.

5. To make the little blossoms, embroider the inner dot with the Wineberry Dark, the five outer dots with the Nutmeg Medium and the leaves in lazy-daisy using the Pine floss.

6. For the Lattice design, referring to the pattern, embroider as follows: embroider the lattice areas in straight stitch using color 108 Lavender Light. Also using this color, embroider the petal center lines in straight-stitch.

7. Stitch the stems in back-stitch using 243 Grass Green Medium. Also using this color, embroider the little leaf in lazy-daisy stitch.

8. Referring to the pattern, embroider the flower petals and the flower tops using the two shades of glacier blue in stem- or outline-stitch.

9. Embroider the flower pistils using the 1002 Antique Gold Light in French knots with tails.

After completing the embroidery, wash to remove markings and press the finished pillowcases.

Cheryl's tip:

Refer to the Yellow Blossoms Embroidered Bed Linens project for a tip on placing the pillowcases securely in an embroidery hoop.

PROJECT 3

Dainty Handkerchief

Here is a quick and easy project that can be worked up in a jiffy. I used a pre-purchased hankie for this project, but you can easily make your own hankie by cutting an 11-inch square of lightweight cotton or linen fabric and stitching a double hem (refer to Chapter 4 for hemming instructions). Add handmade lace to the edges for an elegant touch.

You can then use the hankie as it was intended, but I prefer to use them for decorative purposes. Use it as a simple doily, or make a fashion statement by having it peek out from the pocket of a nice ladies' business suit for a delightfully feminine touch.

The use of pearl cotton rather than 6-strand floss cuts down on time (no separating of strands involved) and gives the stitching a pearly luster. If you prefer to use floss, use 3 strands in your needle to embroider this design.

DIFFICULTY LEVEL:

MAKING THE PROJECT

1. Trace the design using washable pencil on all four corners of the hankie, placing the design about 1/2 inch from the edges.

2. Embroider the stems in backstitch using Spruce Light.

MATERIALS NEEDED:

- One pre-made cotton or linen handkerchief
- One ball each of Pearl Cotton #8 in the following colors:

Anchor#	DMC#		Color Name
206	564		Spruce Light
9	352		Salmon Medium Light
305	726		Topaz Light

STITCHES USED:

Backstitch   Lazy-daisy   French knot

---

3. Stitch the leaves in lazy-daisy using the Spruce Light thread.

4. Work the petals in lazy-daisy using the Topaz Light thread.

5. And finally, work the flower centers in French knot using the Salmon Medium Light thread.

PROJECT 4

Pink Lattice Doily

The inspiration for this project came from a sweet little runner I found in an antiques store. The fabric had disintegrated into a heap full of holes, but the embroidery was still bright and clear (even though the colors of the original embroidery were purple and black and not what I would deem suitable for today's décor). I have updated the colors, using soft rose, wine, and juniper green. The project is quick to stitch, and the colors can be easily changed to suit any room in your home.

DIFFICULTY LEVEL:

MATERIALS NEEDED:

- 20-by-20-inch square of pre-washed white oxford cloth or other even-weave fabric
- 36 inches of pre-washed flat lace trim
- White all-purpose thread for hemming and attaching the lace
- One 10-gram ball of pearl cotton #8 in the following colors:

Anchor#	DMC#		Color Name
214	368		Juniper Light
216	367		Juniper Medium
307	783		Topaz Medium
894	224		Rose Wine Medium Light
970	3726		Wineberry Medium Dark

FINISHED SIZE:

19 by 19 inches

Cheryl's tip:

If you prefer to use six-strand floss rather than pearl cotton, embroider using four of the six strands in your needle.

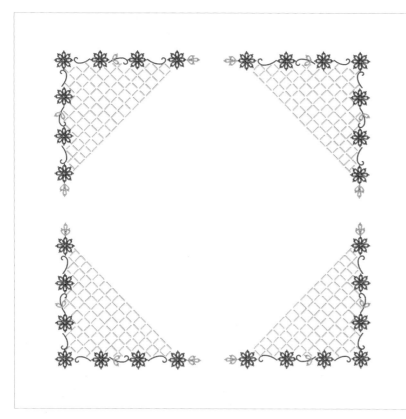

Marking the embroidery design on the fabric.

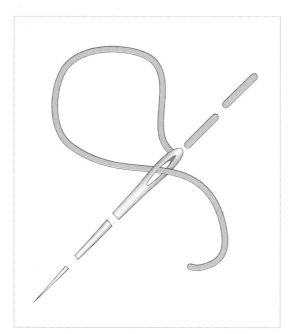

Embroidering the lattice areas.

MAKING THE PROJECT

1. Using a water-soluble pencil, mark a 14-1/2-inch square in the center of the white fabric. Do not cut at this time. Edge-finish the raw edges of the fabric using a machine zigzag stitch or using a liquid sealant.

2. Trace one embroidery motif in each corner, inside the marked square, placing the outermost edges of the motifs exactly 1 inch from the marked lines. Place the fabric in an embroidery hoop.

3. Embroider along the lattice lines in the running stitch, using Rose Wine Medium Light. You'll want to make certain you don't tug the lattice thread too tightly when working these areas. Keep an even tension to avoid puckering the fabric.

4. Embroider the flower stems in stem-stitch, using the Juniper Medium.

5. Embroider the leaves, using the Juniper Light, in the lazy-daisy (single-chain) stitch.

6. Embroider the flowers in lazy-daisy stitch, using Wineberry Medium Dark.

7. The flower centers are embroidered with French knots, using Topaz Medium.

8. After the stitching has been completed, trim away the fabric along the lines you marked in Step 1. Fold under each edge of the fabric 1/4 inch twice around all four sides to make a double hem. Stitch the hem in place by hand, using the white all-purpose thread.

9. Hand- or machine-stitch the lace trim to the doily to complete the project.

Full-sized pattern

Yellow Luncheon Set

With the warm colors of sun and sky, this project seems to have come straight from a country village in Italy. Because the project is worked in only one color of thread, changing colors to suit your own preferences is a breeze.

To make short work of the project, purchase a tablecloth in any size and as many napkins as you need. This project was designed for tablecloths with square corners; therefore, I don't recommend using a round or oval tablecloth with this pattern.

The materials listed here are enough for a 54-by-54-inch tablecloth and four napkins. To make a larger tablecloth, trace the corners as you would for the 54-inch tablecloth and lengthen the straight blue line that connects the corners. Because the four corners remain the same, you do not need to add additional pearl cotton to your shopping list. However, plan for additional napkins by adding one extra skein of pearl cotton for every four added napkins.

I have rated this a two-needle project only because it is time-consuming to complete the entire set. The actual embroidery is simple and easy to stitch.

DIFFICULTY LEVEL:

MATERIALS NEEDED:

- Cotton or linen tablecloth, 54-inch square
- Four 18-inch napkins to match
- Six skeins of Cobalt Blue Medium #3 pearl cotton
- Anchor #130 or DMC color #809

Cheryl's tip:

If you crochet and would like a coordinating edging, purchase enough additional pearl cotton to make the edging.

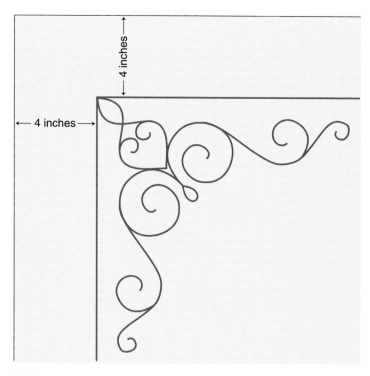

Tablecloth pattern placed 4-inches from edge of cloth.

Pattern placed 1-inch from napkin edges.

MAKING THE PROJECT

1. Enlarge the tablecloth pattern 200% on a photocopier. (Pattern has been reduced 50% to fit the size of the pages in this book.)

2. Using a washable pencil, trace the enlarged pattern on each corner of the tablecloth, placing it 4 inches from the hemmed edge of the cloth. Join the corner motifs by marking a line between them using a ruler or yardstick.

3. Trace the napkin pattern on one corner of each napkin, placing it 1 inch from the corner. The napkin pattern is given full-size.

4. Cut a length of pearl cotton slightly longer than your arm and thread a sharp needle with an eye large enough to accommodate the heavy thread. Embroider the marked designs using the chain-stitch.

5. If desired, crochet a coordinating edging using the extra pearl cotton. Consult existing crochet pattern booklets for instructions.

Pattern for tablecloth corners—reduced 50%.
Enlarge 200% on photocopier before tracing.

Full-sized pattern for napkins.

White-on-White Doily

WHITE-ON-WHITE SATIN-STITCHED LINENS HAVE BEEN A FAVORITE OF BRIDES FOR GENERATIONS AND A SET OF THEM WOULD MAKE A LOVELY BRIDAL SHOWER GIFT. EASY-BUT-ELEGANT DRAWN THREAD EMBROIDERY MAKES THIS SMALL DOILY A TREAT TO STITCH. THE SATIN-STITCHING WILL REQUIRE A BIT OF PRACTICE, WHICH IS WHY I GAVE THIS PROJECT A 2-NEEDLE RATING.

MATERIALS NEEDED:

- 15-by-15-inch piece of Zweigart "Newcastle" 40-count even-weave linen, color #100 (white)
- 2 skeins of White 6-strand Anchor or DMC embroidery floss
- 1-1/2 yards flat white lace
- White all-purpose thread

DIFFICULTY LEVEL:

Cheryl's tip:

If you're unsure of yourself and prefer not to work any drawn-thread patterns, you can fill the gaps with 1/4-inch wide ribbon instead! Simply weave the ribbon under and over 4 threads of the fabric and secure the ends by tucking them under the fabric and stitching them down at the ends.

MAKING THE PROJECT:

Note: Two strands of the 6-strand floss are used for all of the embroidery.

1. Pull a thread from the fabric exactly 2 inches from each edge. Pull an additional 5 alongside the resulting gap towards the inside of the fabric.

2. Referring to the chapter detailing hem-stitching and drawn-thread work, work the gaps, using the white all-purpose thread, in bundles of 4 threads in any drawn-thread pattern you choose.

3. Transfer the embroidery pattern to the fabric. You'll place one motif at each cor-ner, inside the drawn work area, plus one in the center.

4. Embroider the flower stems in stem- or outline-stitch using 2 strands of the white floss. Embroider the flowers and leaves in satin-stitch, also using 2 strands of floss. Stitch in the direction shown in figure below for best results.

5. After completing the embroidery, turn under the raw edges of the fabric and attach the lace using the white all-purpose thread to complete the project.

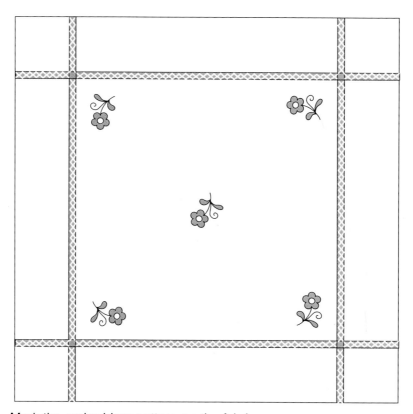

Mark the embroidery pattern on the fabric.

Direction of satin-stitching.

Full-sized embroidery motif.

PROJECT 7

Redwork Hearts Centerpiece

REDWORK HAS EXPERIENCED QUITE A REVIVAL RECENTLY; IT SEEMS TO BE EVERY-WHERE. HERE'S A SIMPLE PROJECT FOR YOUR TABLE. THE PATTERN IS EMBROIDERED IN VARIEGATED SIX-STRAND FLOSS. ALTHOUGH YOU CAN EASILY SUBSTITUTE A SOLID RED, I HOPE YOU'LL DECIDE TO STAY WITH THE VARIEGATED FLOSS BECAUSE IT GIVES THE PROJECT A TEXTURED LOOK.

THE PROJECT CAN BE EASILY ADAPTED TO LARGER OR SMALLER SIZES BY ADDING OR DECREASING THE NUMBER OF "HEART UNITS" ALONG THE SIDES. IT CAN ALSO BE WORKED AS A RECTANGLE BY VARYING THE NUMBER OF HEART UNITS.

NOTE THAT THE PROJECT IS WORKED ON WOOL FABRIC. THE RECOMMENDED METHOD OF LAUNDERING IS TO HAVE IT PROFESSIONALLY DRY-CLEANED. BUT LUCKILY, TABLE CENTERPIECES ARE USED FOR DECORATIVE PURPOSES AND RARELY REQUIRE CLEANING.

ANOTHER OPTION WOULD BE TO WORK THE DESIGN IN BLUE THREAD ON WHITE—APPROPRIATELY KNOWN AS "BLUEWORK." BECAUSE THE MATERIAL NAMED IN THE MATERIALS LIST COMES IN A NATURAL COLOR ONLY, SUBSTITUTE A SIMILAR-COUNT WHITE FABRIC IF STITCH-ING THE DESIGN IN BLUE.

DIFFICULTY LEVEL:

Cheryl's tip:

Read instructions carefully. Don't hem the fabric until after you mark the design on the cloth.

MATERIALS NEEDED:

- One 30-inch square of Zweigart 3349 Wool Hardanger cloth, 22-count in color #101
- Three skeins of six-strand embroidery floss
- Variegated red: Anchor color #1206 or DMC #115
- 4 yards of beige 2-1/2-inch Cluny Lace or other chunky lace

FINISHED SIZE:

Approximately 25 by 25 inches

MAKING THE PROJECT

1. Beginning at the upper left corner of the fabric and working from left to right, trace the embroidery design using washable pencil or tailor's chalk. Start with a corner unit, placing the design 2-1/2 inches from the edges of the fabric.

2. Continue adding heart units until the marked area contains eleven heart units (or desired length) and then trace another corner. Repeat for all four sides. The design will not be squared; it will be very much off-centered. We will fix this in a moment.

3. Mark a line around all four sides of the marked design, 2 inches from the outside edge of the design. Cut along this line and discard the excess fabric. Your fabric will now have the embroidery design centered nicely.

4. Zigzag along the raw outer edges of the fabric, using matching all-purpose thread to prevent fraying. Turn under the edges of the fabric 1/4-inch twice to make a doubled hem. Stitch the hem in place by hand or machine, using matching all-purpose thread.

5. Cut a length of floss the length of your arm and separate into two groups of three strands. Using one group of three strands in your needle, embroider the hearts in stem-stitch. Using the lazy-daisy stitch, embroider the little blossoms, the heart tips, and the corner sprigs also using three strands of floss.

6. Carefully remove any markings that may show beyond the embroidery, using a white eraser or damp cotton swab. If you used tailor's chalk to mark your design, brush away the chalk markings. Try not to wet the wool fabric.

7. Referring to Chapter 4, attach lace to the outer edges of the centerpiece to complete.

Laying out the embroidery design.

Corner Unit   Heart Unit

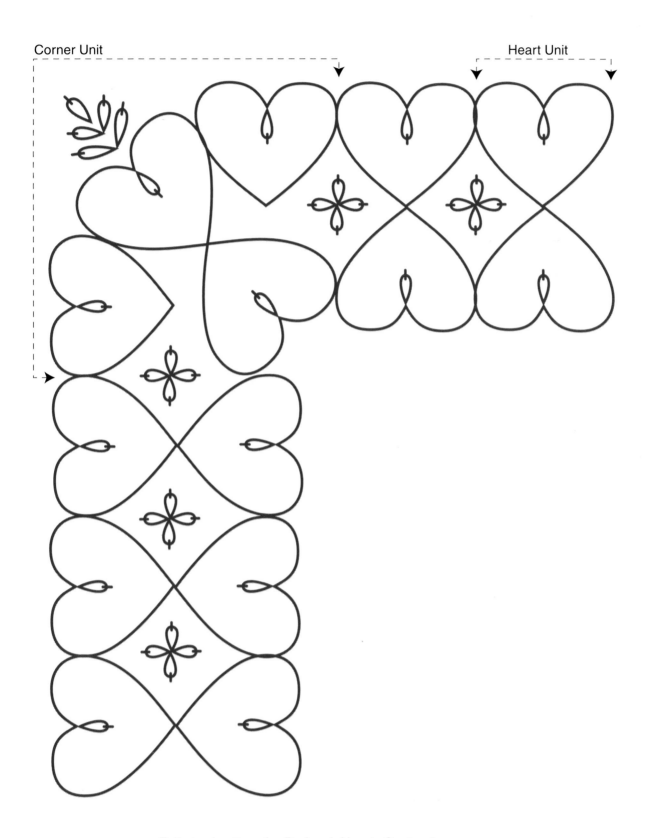

Full-sized pattern for Redwork Hearts Centerpiece.

Reverse Redwork Pincushion

REVERSE REDWORK IS SIMPLE A REVERSAL OF THE COLORS USED IN TRADITIONAL REDWORK EMBROIDERY. INSTEAD OF STITCHING IN RED THREAD ON WHITE FABRIC, THE STITCHING IS WORKED IN WHITE THREAD ON RED FABRIC.

THE SIMPLE FLORAL SPRAY USED ON THIS LITTLE PINCUSHION IS ADAPTABLE TO NAPKINS, SACHETS OR OTHER ITEMS. IT MAY ALSO BE USED IN REPEAT TO FORM A BAND, AS IN THE TEA COZY PROJECT FEATURED ELSEWHERE IN THIS BOOK.

MATERIALS NEEDED:

- Two 8-by-8-inch squares of Zweigart "Jubilee" 28-count even-weave linen, in Christmas Red
- 1 ball of Anchor or DMC Size 8 Pearl Cotton, white
- Red all-purpose thread
- 20-inch length of white pre-gathered lace trim
- Polyester fiberfill for stuffing

FINISHED SIZE OF PINCUSHION:

6 inches in diameter

DIFFICULTY LEVEL:

MAKING THE PROJECT

1. Trace the embroidery design on the center of one red square of fabric using a water-soluble pencil (white or yellow works best on this dark fabric). Do not mark the circle at this time.

2. Embroider the flower and leaf outlines in stem or outline stitch using the white pearl cotton.

3. Embroider the flower dots inside each petal in French knots.

4. After completing the embroidery, cut out the circle using the pattern, cutting along the solid line only (the dotted line is the stitching line).

5. Stitch the lace to the edges of the embroidered circle using the all-purpose thread.

6. Place the embroidered circle against the remaining square of fabric, right sides together. Stitch around the circle along the lace line, leaving open between the two dots indicated on the pattern.

7. Trim away the excess fabric from the second square so that it is flush with the embroidered circle. Seal the edges with a permanent seam sealant or zigzag over the raw edges. This will keep them from fraying. Clip the curves so the pincushion will lie flat after turning.

8. Turn the pincushion right side out through the opening left in the seam. Press. Stuff with fiberfill.

9. Hand-stitch the turning opening closed to complete the project.

leave open for turning

Full-sized embroidery pattern.

Redwork Coverlet

DON'T LET THE PROJECT'S THREE-NEEDLE RATING INTIMIDATE YOU! THE EMBROIDERY IS ACTUALLY QUITE EASY—THE RATING IS BASED SOLELY ON THE SIZE OF THE PROJECT AND THE LENGTH OF TIME NEEDED TO COMPLETE IT.

THIS PROJECT IS BASED ON A "BLOCK-OF-THE-MONTH" PLAN. FOR THOSE PRESSED FOR TIME, PLAN ON COMPLETING ONE BLOCK EACH MONTH, WITH AN EXTRA WEEK OR TWO SPENT ASSEMBLING AND MACHINE QUILTING (IF DESIRED) THE PROJECT. THOSE WITH A BIT OF EXTRA TIME WILL FIND THEY CAN COMPLETE ONE OR TWO BLOCKS PER WEEK. I ALLOWED MYSELF ONE WEEK PER BLOCK.

IF YOU DON'T CARE MUCH FOR RED AND WHITE, FEEL FREE TO CHANGE THE COLORS TO ANYTHING YOUR HEART DESIRES. THE PROJECT WOULD LOOK EQUALLY LOVELY IN OTHER COLOR COMBINATIONS—BUT BE SURE TO HAVE A STARK CONTRAST BETWEEN DARK AND LIGHT, FOR BEST RESULTS.

DIFFICULTY LEVEL:

MATERIALS NEEDED:

- 2 yards of white 100% cotton broadcloth
- 16 skeins of red 6-strand embroidery floss
- Anchor color #19 Burgundy Medium or DMC color #304
- 1/2 yard red & white checkered fabric for inner border
- White all-purpose thread for assembly and red for binding
- 1 piece EACH batting and backing (lining) fabric measuring 52 by 56 inches
- 6 yards of red double-fold binding

FINISHED SIZE OF THE COVERLET:

48 by 52 inches

FINISHED BLOCK SIZE:

8 by 8 inches

Cheryl's tip:

Read instructions carefully. Bear in mind that quilting this project is completely optional and it would look just as pretty simply lined and used as a summer coverlet. For more information on quilting, refer to some of the excellent quilting books in your local bookstore.

MAKING THE PROJECT

Cut the following from the white broadcloth:

- 12 squares measuring 9 by 9 inches for blocks (will be trimmed to 8-1/2 by 8-1/2 later)
- 8 strips measuring 2-1/2 by 8-1/2 inches for vertical sashing strips
- 3 strips measuring 2-1/2 by 28-1/2 inches for horizontal sashing strips
- 2 strips measuring 2-1/2 by 38-1/2 inches for white vertical inside border
- 2 strips measuring 2-1/2 by 32-1/2 inches for white horizontal inside border
- 2 strips measuring 8-1/2 by 46-1/2 inches for white vertical outer border
- 2 strips measuring 8-1/2 by 52-1/2 inches for white horizontal outer border

Cut the following from the red & white checkered print:

- 2 strips measuring 2-1/2 by 42-1/2 inches for vertical border
- 2 strips measuring 2-1/2 by 36-1/2 inches for horizontal border

1. Trace one block design on each of the 12 white squares using a water-soluble pencil, centering the design on each block.

2. Cut a length of embroidery floss no longer than your arm. Divide this into 3 units having 2 strands each. Embroider the blocks, one at a time, using the guide below:

January: all embroidery is done in outline- or stem-stitch.

February: use outline- or stem-stitch, and French knots for the dots in flower centers.

March: use outline- or stem-stitch except along dotted lines, which are worked in running stitch.

April: use outline- or stem-stitch except for leaves, which are worked in lazy-daisy.

May: work leaves and stems in outline- or stem-stitch, work flowers in straight-stitch and dots in flower centers in French knots.

June: use outline- or stem-stitch, French knots for dots in flower centers, and straight-stitch for the band detail on watering can.

July: work in stem- or outline-stitch, work small sprays in fern-stitch and details at flower centers in seed-stitch.

August: use stem- or outline-stitch and French knots for flower dots.

September: use stem- or outline-stitch, French knots for dots in flower centers.

October: use stem- or outline-stitch, French knots at flower centers, and straight stitch for short basket details.

November: work stems and bow in outline-stitch or stem-stitch and wheat berries in lazy-daisy.

December: work outlines in stem- or outline-stitch, holly berry dots in French knots and leaf details in running-stitch.

3. Trim down all finished blocks to measure 8-1/2 by 8-1/2 inches and load your sewing machine with the all-purpose thread to prepare for assembly, using the pieces cut in steps one and two. Use a 1/4-inch seam allowance for all assembly.

4. Referring to the illustration, stitch the first 3 blocks alternately with two of the vertical sashing strips to make a row. Repeat to make 4 rows.

5. Stitch the five rows to the four horizontal sashing strips to make the coverlet center. Stitch the white vertical borders to the long sides of the coverlet center and the horizontal borders strips to the top and bottom edges.

6. Stitch the red border to the coverlet center, stitching the vertical strips to the sides and the horizontal strips to the top and bottom edges. Repeat with the wide outer borders. This completes the coverlet top.

7. Layer the coverlet with the batting and backing fabric and hand- or pin-baste the layers together to prepare for quilting. Hand or machine quilt as desired.

8. Stitch 1/8 inch from the raw edges of the coverlet top and trim away the excess batting and backing fabric. Bind the coverlet with the red bias tape using matching red thread to complete the project.

ABC Sampler

THIS DAINTY, DELICATE SAMPLER IS VERY EASY TO MAKE AND USES JUST THREE BASIC STITCHES: BACKSTITCH, FRENCH KNOT AND SINGLE CHAIN. THE TWO-NEEDLE RATING IS BASED ON TIME REQUIRED TO COMPLETE, RATHER THAN DEGREE OF DIFFICULTY.

ON THE FOLLOWING PAGES YOU'LL ALSO FIND TWO OTHER PROJECTS—MONO-GRAMMED SACHETS AND NAPKINS—WHICH SHARE THE SAME ALPHABET AS THE SAMPLER. OTHER CREATIVE USES FOR THE ALPHABET PATTERNS WOULD BE MONOGRAMS FOR SHEETS, BABY ITEMS, AND LINEN GUEST TOW-ELS. ALL OF THESE WOULD MAKE GREAT TAKE-ALONG PROJECTS WHEN TRAVELLING OR COM-MUTING!

MATERIALS NEEDED:

- 18-by-20-inch piece of Zweigart "Newcastle" 40-count even-weave linen, color #100 (white)
- Frame and mat
- 1 skein of the following 6-strand embroi-dery floss:

Anchor#	DMC#		Color Name
146	322		Delft Blue
875	3817		Pine Light
877	3815		Pine Medium
311	3855		Tangerine Very Light
1022	760		Peony Medium Light
1025	347		Peony Medium Dark

FINISHED SIZE OF EMBROIDERED AREA:

Approximately 7 by 8 inches

DIFFICULTY LEVEL:

MAKING THE PROJECT

Note: Two strands of the 6-strand floss are used throughout.

1. Edge-finish the piece of linen to keep it from fraying while working the embroidery. You can use either a liquid seam sealant, or zigzag over the edges with all-purpose thread.

2. Trace the embroidery design in the cen-ter if the rectangle of linen using a water-soluble pencil.

3. Embroider the letters in backstitch using the Delft Blue floss.

4. Embroider the lighter green leaves in sin-gle chain using the Pine Light floss. The darker green leaves are embroidered in the same stitch using the Pine Medium floss.

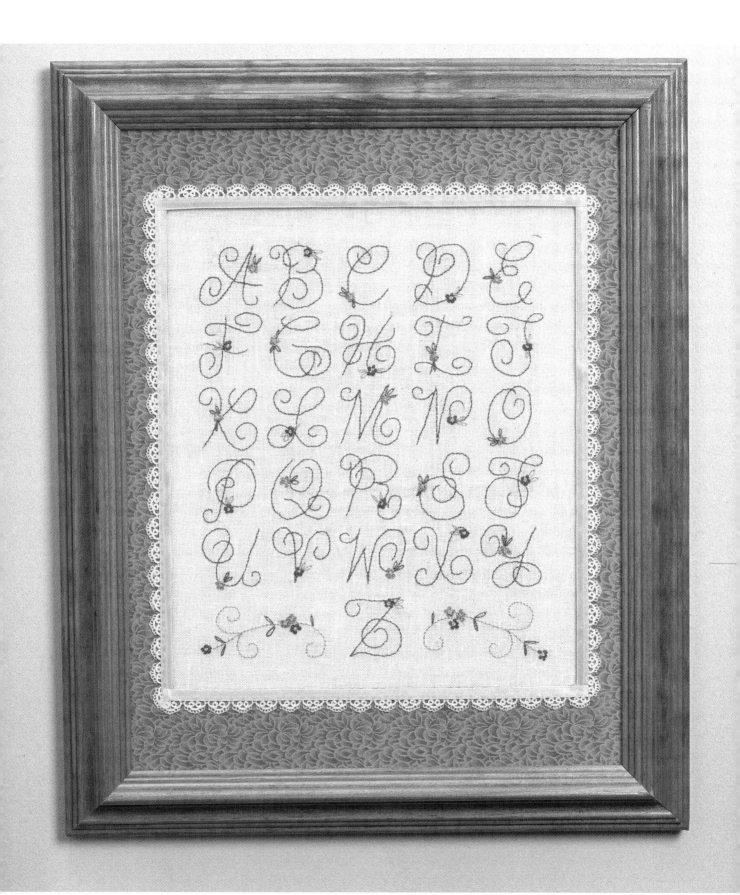

5. Embroider the light flowers in French knots using the Peony Medium Light floss. The dark flowers are embroidered in the same manner using the Peony Medium Dark floss.

6. Embroider the flower centers in French knots using the Tangerine Very Light floss.

7. The vines at the bottom of the sampler are worked in backstitch using the Pine Light floss and the leaves are single-chain using the Pine Medium. Embroider the flowers on the vines in the same manner as those on the letters.

8. Mat (if desired) and frame the finished sampler.

ABC Sachets

This project uses the same alphabet as the ABC Sampler shown on the previous pages. Although a letter is shown inside the circle, substitute any letter needed, tracing from the full-size sampler pattern.

The floss colors indicated are the same as those used on the sampler—feel free to make substitutions to suit your needs. The sample sachets shown in the photo use the threads in a variety of color arrays.

DIFFICULTY LEVEL:

MATERIALS NEEDED:

- (2) 6-by-6-inch squares of Zweigart "Newcastle" 40-count even-weave linen, color #100 (white) for each sachet
- White all-purpose thread
- 20-inch length of white medium-width rick rack
- Stuffing and/or potpourri
- 1 skein of the following 6-strand embroidery floss:

Anchor#	DMC#		Color Name
146	322		Delft Blue
875	3817		Pine Light
877	3815		Pine Medium
311	3855		Tangerine Very Light
1022	760		Peony Medium Light
1025	347		Peony Medium Dark

FINISHED SIZE OF SACHET:

4 by 4 inches

MAKING THE PROJECT

Note: Two strands of the 6-strand floss are used throughout.

1, Trace the embroidery design and desired monogram at the center of one white square of linen using a water-soluble pencil.

2. Embroider the circle outside the monogram in desired color using the feather-stitch.

3. Embroider the lettering in desired color using backstitch.

4. Embroider the flower centers in desired color in French knots.

5. Embroider the flower petals in desired color in French knots.

6. Embroider the leaves in single chain (lazy-daisy) using either of the green floss colors.

7. Trace the sachet cutting pattern on the embroidered square, centering the embroidery within the inside square. Cut out along the solid line (do not cut along the dashed line—this is the stitching line).

8. Attach the rick rack around the edges of the sachet using the white thread. Center the rick rack along the dashed line.

9. After stitching the rick rack, place the embroidered square and the remaining square together, right sides facing. Stitch along the dashed lines (indicated on the reverse side by the stitching line for the rick rack), leaving the area between the two dots unstitched.

10. Trim away the excess from the second square of fabric, making them even with those of the embroidered piece. Clip the corners of the sachet to make them lie flat and turn the sachet right-side out through the opening.

11. Stuff the sachet with fiberfill, potpourri or mixture of both. Hand-stitch the opening closed using an invisible stitch.

Full-size embroidery pattern for sachet.

leave open for turning

Full-size sachet pattern. Leave open between dots for turning.

ABC Napkins

THESE NAPKINS USE THE SAME ALPHABET AS THE ABC SAMPLER AND THE SAME CIRCLE AS THE SACHETS SHOWN ON THE PREVIOUS PAGES.

THE NAPKINS LOOK SENSATIONAL PAIRED WITH FINE CHINA AND A PLAIN WHITE TABLECLOTH. OF COURSE, YOU CAN ALSO EMBROIDER THE MONOGRAM ONTO THE CORNERS OR CENTER SIDES OF THE TABLECLOTH, BUT IT'S UP TO YOU. IF DESIRED, OMIT THE CIRCLE AND USE THE MONOGRAM ALONE.

THE PLACEMENT OF THE MONOGRAM WILL DEPEND ON HOW YOU PREFER TO FOLD THE NAPKINS, SO BE SURE TO READ THE INSTRUCTIONS BEFORE MARKING THE FABRIC.

DIFFICULTY LEVEL:

MATERIALS NEEDED:

- 20-by-20-inch piece of Zweigart "Newcastle" 40-count even-weave linen, color #100 (white) for each napkin
- White all-purpose thread
- 2-1/4 yards flat lace trim for each napkin (optional)
- 1 skein of the following 6-strand embroidery floss:

Anchor#	DMC#		Color Name
146	322		Delft Blue
875	3817		Pine Light
877	3815		Pine Medium
311	3855		Tangerine Very Light
1022	760		Peony Medium Light
1025	347		Peony Medium Dark

FINISHED SIZE OF NAPKINS:

19 by 19 inches

MAKING THE PROJECT

Note: Two strands of the 6-strand floss are used throughout.

1. Turn under the raw edges around all 4 sides of the napkins 1/4 inch twice to make a doubled folded hem. Stitch the hem in place using the all-purpose thread (by hand or machine).

2. If desired, add lace to the edges of the napkins, stitching it in place with the all-purpose thread.

3. Transfer the monogram and circle onto one corner of the napkin using a water-soluble pencil. The position of the transfer will depend on how you prefer to fold the napkin. If you normally fold your napkins in a rectangular shape, trace the monogram as shown on the left in the illustration. If you prefer to have the monogram at the point of a corner, trace it as shown on the right. Whichever direction you place them, space them no more than 1/2 inch from the napkin edges.

4. Using the desired colors, embroider the circle in feather-stitch. Embroider the monogram in backstitch, and the flower and flower center in French knots. Embroider the leaves in single-chain (lazy-daisy) stitch.

Repeat for the number of napkins needed.

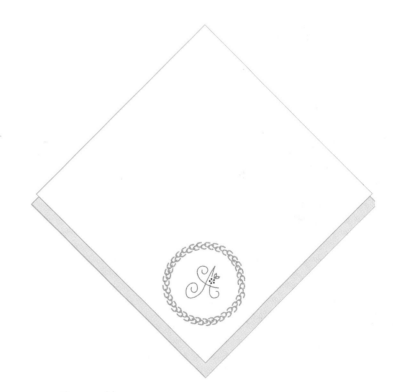

Two methods for placing the monogram on the napkins.

Blue Nightgown and Slippers

THE ELEGANCE OF SATIN STITCH IS UNMATCHED BY ANY OTHER EMBROIDERY STITCH. SATIN STITCH HAS A SMOOTH "SATINY" SURFACE (HENCE ITS NAME) BUT REQUIRES AN INVESTMENT OF BOTH TIME AND MATERIALS—THIS STITCH WILL EAT UP YOUR FLOSS QUICKLY AND SOME PRACTICE IS REQUIRED.

THE PROJECT CAN BE MADE FROM A PURCHASED NIGHTGOWN, OR FROM ONE YOU MAKE YOURSELF FROM A COMMERCIAL SEWING PATTERN (BE SURE TO NOTE THE TIP IN STEP 1). IF YOU NEED TO ADJUST THE SIZE OF THE YOKE EMBROIDERY PATTERN, ENLARGE OR REDUCE IT ON A PHOTOCOPIER TO SUIT YOUR NEEDS.

MATERIALS NEEDED:

- White flannel nightgown, either purchased or made from commercial pattern
- Pair of purchased white terry slippers
- Skeins of the following 6-strand embroidery floss

Amount	Anchor#	DMC#		Color Name
2	128	775		Cobalt Blue Light
2	977	334		Sea Blue Medium
1	164	3842		Sapphire Dark
1	289	307		Canary Yellow Med. Light

FINISHED SIZE OF SET:

Any size desired

DIFFICULTY LEVEL:

Cheryl's tip:

If you are making your own nightgown from this project, cut out all pieces from the commercial pattern except the front yoke. Cut a rectangle of the fabric slightly larger than the yoke pattern. Trace the yoke onto the rectangle of fabric without cutting it out and embroider it. After completing the embroidery, cut out the yoke and sew the nightgown together according to the pattern directions. This tip makes it easier to stitch the yoke, and you won't have to keep the entire nightie on your lap as you stitch!

MAKING THE PROJECT

Note: Two strands of the 6-strand floss are used for all of the embroidery.

1. Mark the nightgown embroidery pattern onto the yoke of the gown using a water-soluble pencil: align the center line of the 1/2 pattern with the center of the yoke and trace the first side. Then, flip the pattern and trace the reverse side.

2. Referring to the stitch key, embroider the yoke. The stitches used in the project are satin-stitch, backstitch, chain-stitch, single-chain and lazy-daisy.

Nightgown Yoke Stitch Key

Chain-stitch - color 128
Chain-stitch - color 977
Backstitch - color 164
Single Chain - color 164
Satin-stitch - color 977
Satin-stitch - color 128
Satin-stitch - color 289

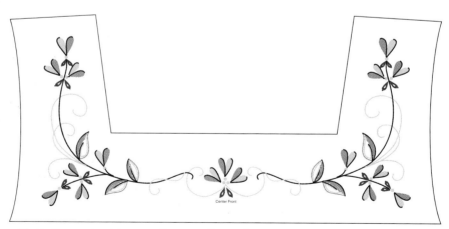

Mark the embroidery pattern on the yoke.

3. To make the slippers, transfer the pattern to each slipper and embroider as indicated on the stitch key.

Slipper Pattern

Slipper Stitch Key

———————— Backstitch - color 164

Single Chain - color 1977

Satin-stitch - color 289

Center Front

1/2 of the yoke pattern.

Delicate Chrysanthemum Pillow

Embroidered using just two stitches—backstitch and lazy-daisy—this project is quick to stitch and easy to finish. You can personalize the pillow by adding the monogram of a special friend for a gift that will be forever cherished. Use the alphabet for the ABC Sampler, placing the desired letter in the center of the circle.

DIFFICULTY LEVEL:

MATERIALS NEEDED:

- Two 14-inch squares of pre-washed Zweigart 3217 "Edinburgh" 36-count linen, color #101 (an off-white) or another even-weave fabric
- 1 yard of wide-gathered lace trim
- Natural color all-purpose thread for assembling the pillow
- Polyester fiberfill for stuffing
- One skein each of six-strand cotton floss in the following colors:

Anchor#	DMC#		Color Name
890	436		Brass Light
843	3053		Fern Green
846	3051		Fern Green Dark
1016	3727		Antique Mauve Light
1018	3726		Antique Mauve Dark
1028	3685		Raspberry Medium Dark

Making the Project

1. Edge-finish the raw edges of the fabric using a machine zigzag stitch or using a liquid sealant. Fold one of the squares into quarters, and press to mark the center lines. Unfold the square.

2. Trace the entire embroidery design onto the square of fabric you just pressed into quarters. Do not trace the circular line or the centering line; align the centering line along one of the creases. Place the marked fabric in an embroidery hoop.

3. Use two strands of the six-strand floss for all embroidery.

4. Embroider along the stem lines in back-stitch, using the Fern Green Dark. Keep an even tension to avoid puckering the fabric. Embroider the leaves in lazy-daisy stitch, using Fern Green.

5. Embroider the center flower petal in lazy-daisy stitch, using Raspberry Medium Dark. Embroider the petal on each side of the center petal in Antique Mauve Dark. Embroider the outermost petals, using the Antique Mauve Light.

6. The flower centers are embroidered with French knots in Brass Light.

7. After the stitching has been completed, mark a circle 1-1/2 inches from the outside edges of the embroidered wreath. Trim away the fabric along the lines. Attach lace using the all-purpose thread.

8. Place the trimmed circle and the remaining piece of fabric, right sides together. Stitch, leaving a 5-inch opening for turning. Trim backing fabric even with circle.

9. Clip curves and turn pillow right-side out. Stuff with fiberfill. Hand-stitch the turning opening closed, using all-purpose thread to complete the project.

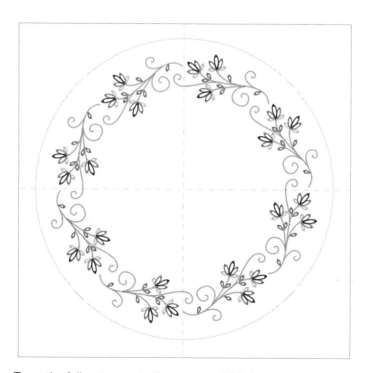

Trace the full pattern onto the square of fabric.

1/2 of full-sized pattern

Coffee and Tea Towels

Here's a quick-to-stitch project that would make a lovely hostess gift for a special friend. The nifty navy on white fabric is also available in other colors, such as mauve on white, celadon (green) on white and red on white. Check with your local needlework shop for more information on colors.

DIFFICULTY LEVEL:

MATERIALS NEEDED (FOR TWO TOWELS):

- 1/2 yard of Zweigart "Diana" even-weave fabric, color #15 navy/white
- 1 yard flat lace trim (optional)
- 1 spool white all-purpose thread
- 1 skein of the following 6-strand embroidery floss:

Anchor#	DMC#		Color Name
150	336	■	Delft Blue Dark
146	322	▬	Deft Blue
289	307	▬	Canary Yellow Medium

FINISHED SIZE OF EACH TOWEL:

Approximately 18 by 27 inches

MAKING THE PROJECT

Note: Three strands of the 6-strand floss are used throughout.

1. Cut the fabric in half along the center to make two pieces measuring 18 by 22-1/2 inches. Turn under the raw edges of the fabric 1/4 inch twice to make a doubled hem and stitch hem in place using the all-purpose thread.

2. Transfer the embroidery markings to the fabric using a water-soluble pencil. Center the design along on short end of each hemmed towel, two inches from the edge.

3. Separate a length of the Delft Blue dark floss into two units having three strands each. Embroider the outlines of the pots and the lettering in stem or outline stitch using this color. Embroider the flower centers in French knots.

Full-sized embroidery patterns for coffee and tea towels.

4. Using the same number of strands of the Delft Blue, embroider the pot details in stem- or outline-stitch. Embroider the steam in running stitch. Embroider the leaves in single chain (lazy-daisy) stitch.

5. Using the Canary Yellow Medium Light, embroider the flower petals in lazy-daisy stitch.

6. Stitch optional lace to embroidered short end of towel using the all-purpose thread.

Circular Daisy Centerpiece

THE TWO-NEEDLE RATING HERE REFLECTS THE NUMBER OF FRENCH KNOTS USED IN THIS PROJECT. WHILE FRENCH KNOTS CAN TAKE A BIT OF PRACTICE TO MASTER, THEY ARE BY NO MEANS DIFFICULT. THINK OF THIS PROJECT AS A SKILL BUILDER! ONCE YOU MASTER YOUR FIRST FRENCH KNOT, YOU'LL BE HOOKED.

DIFFICULTY LEVEL:

MATERIALS NEEDED:

- 25-by-25-inch piece of Zweigart "Newcastle" 40-count even-weave linen, color #100 (white)
- White all-purpose thread
- 3 yards gathered lace trim (optional)
- 1 skein of the following 6-strand embroidery floss:

Anchor#	DMC#		Color Name
875	3817		Pine Light
878	501		Pine Medium Dark
907	783		Saffron Dark
109	209		Lavender Medium Light
86	3608		Orchid Medium Light
78	3803		Antique Rose Dark
131	798		Cobalt Blue Medium

FINISHED SIZE OF CENTERPIECE:

24 inches in diameter

MAKING THE PROJECT

Note: Two strands of the 6-strand floss are used for all stem-stitches and three strands of floss are used for all other embroidery.

1. Fold the square of fabric into quarters and cut out circle using any marking method desired. Edge-finish to prevent fabric from fraying while working the embroidery.

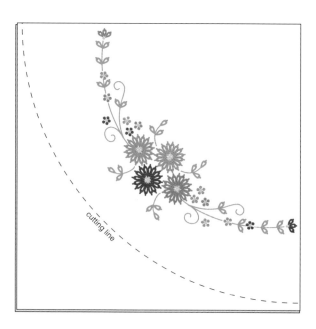

cutting line

2. Cut circle from folded square. Transfer the embroidery pattern to each quarter of the circle using a water-soluble pencil.

3. Using two strands of the Pine Light floss, embroider all of the stem lines in stem- or outline-stitch.

4. Embroider the leaves using three strands of the Pine Medium Dark floss in single chain (lazy-daisy) stitch.

5. Referring to the pattern for color placement, embroider the small blossoms in French knots using 3 strands of floss. All of the centers of the small blossoms are worked in the Saffron Dark floss.

6. Stitch the large flowers in lazy-daisy stitch using 3 strands of floss, referring to the pattern for color placement. The centers of the large flowers are made from 6 Saffron French knots, stitched in a cluster similar to the small blossoms.

7. Turn under and hem the edges of the circle and attach the lace using the all-purpose thread to complete the project.

Full-sized embroidery pattern.

Crewel Place Mat Set

THIS SET IS EMBROIDERED USING JUST ONE STITCH—THE CHAIN-STITCH. BECAUSE A PERFECT CHAIN-STITCH CAN TAKE A LITTLE PRACTICE TO MASTER, I HAVE ASSIGNED THIS GROUP A 3-NEEDLE RATING. REMEMBER NOT TO PULL TOO TIGHTLY WHEN WORKING CHAIN-STITCH OR YOU WILL LOSE THE "RINGS" BY HAVING YOUR TENSION TOO TIGHT. PRACTICE ON SOME SCRAP FABRIC BEFORE STARTING THE PROJECT.

MATERIALS NEEDED:

- 19-by-23-inch rectangle of Zweigart "Belfast" 32-count linen, color #326 (taupe) for each place mat
- 19-by-19-square of the same fabric for each napkin
- 23-by-23-square of the same fabric for bread cloth
- 6-by-6-inch square of the same fabric for each coaster
- All-purpose thread to match fabric
- One skein each of 6-strand embroidery floss in the following colors:

Anchor#	DMC#		Color Name
253	772		Parrot Green Very Light
217	367		Juniper Medium Dark
262	3363		Loden Green Medium
275	746		Citrus Ultra Light
288	445		Canary Yellow Light
339	920		Terra Cotta Medium

DIFFICULTY LEVEL:

MAKING THE PROJECTS

1. To hem the place mats, pull out one thread from the fabric exactly 2-1/4 inches from each edge. Fold under the fabric 1/4 inch, then fold again so the first fold meets the line made in the fabric by the pulled thread. Repeat for all 4 sides, mitering corners. Work hemstitch to secure the hem using the all-purpose thread.

2. Repeat step one for the bread cloth. To hem the napkin, pull a thread one inch from each side of the napkin. Work hemstitching along this line and pull away the remaining outer threads to make a hemstitch fringe.

3. To hem the coaster, pull a thread 1/2 inch from each side and make a hemstitch fringe as for the napkin.

4. Using a water-soluble pencil, transfer the embroidery markings to each piece in the collection as follows:

5. For the napkin and coaster, transfer one single-leaf sprig. Center the sprig for the coaster and place the motif 1/2 inch from edges for the napkin.

6. For the bread cloth, transfer one three-leaf sprig to each corner, placing them about 1-1/2 inches from the edges.

7. For each place mat, transfer one corner unit and one single-leaf motif as shown in the diagram. Place them 2 inches from the edges.

8. Embroider the designs using 3 strands of the six-strand floss in stem-stitch, referring to the color key.

Placement of motif for napkin and coaster.

Placement of motifs for place mat.

Placement of motifs for bread cloth.

Color Key

————	253 Parrot Green Very Light
————	217 Juniper Medium Dark
————	262 Loden Green Medium
————	275 Citrus Ultra Light
————	288 Canary Yellow Light
————	339 Terra Cotta Medium

9. For best results when working the embroidery, stitch all of the outlines first and then fill in the shapes with repeating lines of chain stitch, placed close together.

10. Press the pieces and enjoy!

Single-leaf motif.

Three-leaf motif.

Corner unit.

PROJECT 18

Interlocking Circles Runner

WHETHER USED AS A RUNNER ON A DRESSER OR SIDE TABLE, OR AS A TRAY-CLOTH, THIS SMALL PROJECT WILL BRING OLD-FASHIONED CHARM YOUR ROOM. THE PROJECT WAS INSPIRED BY A VINTAGE PIECE FOUND AT AN ANTIQUES STORE IN OREGON. I HAVE USED FLOSS COLORS SIMILAR TO THE FADED THREADS IN THE ORIGINAL, JUST FOR FUN. OF COURSE, THE COLORS ARE EASILY ADAPTABLE TO YOUR OWN TASTES OR DÉCOR.

DIFFICULTY LEVEL:

MATERIALS NEEDED:

- 15-by-19-inch piece of Zweigart "Lugana Murano" 32-count even-weave fabric, color #100 (white)
- White all-purpose thread
- 2 yards flat, white lace (optional)
- 1 skein of the following 6-strand embroidery floss:

Anchor#	DMC#		Color Name
42	3284	▰	Carmine Rose Medium
890	2875	▰	Brass Light
215	6017	▰	Juniper Medium Light
683	6880	▰	Turf Green
380	5478	▰	Fudge

FINISHED SIZE OF RUNNER:

14 by 18 inches

MAKING THE PROJECT

Note: Two strands of the 6-strand floss are used for backstitch and three strands for all other embroidery. Refer to the color pattern for color placement if necessary.

1. Edge-finish the piece of fabric to keep it from fraying while working the embroidery. You can use either a liquid seam sealant, or zigzag over the edges with all-purpose thread.

2. Trace the embroidery design in the center of each short end of the rectangle of fabric using a water-soluble pencil. Mark the cutting lines on each corner, using the pattern provided, aligning the corner of the pattern with the corner of the fabric. Do not cut out until after the embroidery has been completed.

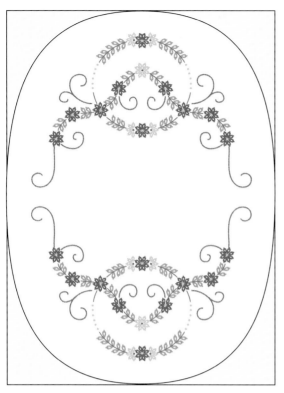

Mark the embroidery and corner patterns on the fabric.

3. Embroider the brown tendrils using two strands of the Fudge floss in backstitch.

4. Embroider the green stem areas in backstitch using 2 strands of the Turf Green floss.

5. Stitch the leaves using 3 strands of the Juniper Medium Light in single chain (lazy-daisy).

6. Embroider the flowers using 3 strands of the Carmine Rose and Brass Light floss, referring to the color pattern in lazy-daisy.

7. Embroider the flower centers using 3 strands of floss in French knots in Carmine Rose Medium for the centers of the brass flowers, and Brass Light for the centers of the Carmine Rose Medium flowers.

Full-sized embroidery pattern.

Center

8. Embroider the Brass Light dots on the circle area using French knots and 3 strands of floss.

9. Cut out the shape of the runner and edge-finish in zigzag using the all-purpose thread. Attach the lace to complete the project.

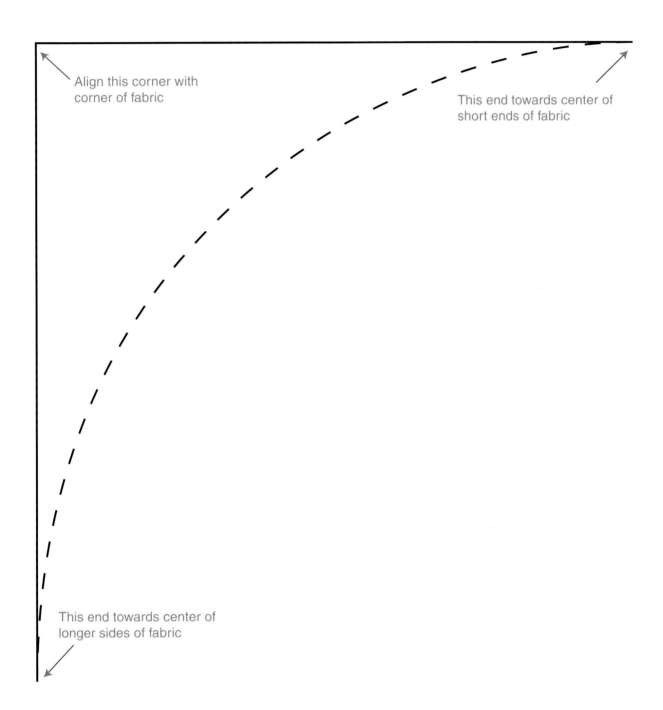

Align this corner with corner of fabric

This end towards center of short ends of fabric

This end towards center of longer sides of fabric

Corner pattern.

PROJECT 19

Home Accent Pillow

THIS SENTIMENTAL LITTLE ACCENT PIL-
LOW WILL BRING A TOUCH OF WARMTH
TO ANY CORNER OF THE HOUSE. WORKED
IN BACKSTITCH, FRENCH KNOTS, OUTLINE-,
SATIN-, AND LAZY-DAISY STITCHES.
ALLOW YOURSELF ABOUT 2 DAYS TO
COMPLETE THE PROJECT, AS THE SATIN-
STITCHING IS A WEE BIT LABOR-INTENSIVE.

DIFFICULTY LEVEL:

MATERIALS NEEDED:

- Two (2) 8-by-15-inch pieces of Zweigart "Edinburgh" 36-count even-weave linen, color #100 (white)
- 1-1/3 yards white loop trim
- White all-purpose thread
- Polyester fiberfill for stuffing
- Skeins indicated of the following 6-strand embroidery floss:

Amount	Anchor#	DMC#		Color Name
2	874	834		Saffron Medium
1	267	470		Avocado Medium
1	265	3348		Avocado Light
1	1027	3722		Rose Wine Medium Dark
1	1002	976		Antique Gold Light
1	145	3755		Delft Blue Light

FINISHED SIZE OF PILLOW:

7 by 14 inches

MAKING THE PROJECT

Note: Two strands of the 6-strand floss are used for all of the embroidery.

1. Edge-finish both of the pieces of fabric by applying seam sealant or machine zigzag stitching.

2. Transfer the embroidery design to the center of one of the pieces of fabric using a water-soluble pencil.

3. Embroider the thick areas of the lettering in satin-stitch using the Saffron Medium floss. Embroider the thin areas in outline- or stem-stitch.

4. Embroider the stems and tendril in stem- or outline-stitching using the Avocado Medium floss. Embroider the leaves in single chain (lazy-daisy) using the Avocado Light floss.

5. Satin-stitch the butterfly wings in Delft Blue and the wing details in Antique Gold Light. Satin-stitch the butterfly body in satin-stitch using the Rose Wine Medium Dark floss. Embroider the antennae in Avocado Light in backstitch.

6. Embroider the centers of the flowers in French knots using the Antique Gold Light. Embroider the flowers in lazy-daisy, having two of them worked in Rose Wine Medium Dark and one worked in the Delft Blue (refer to pattern for color placement).

7. After completing the embroidery, stitch the trim to the outer edges of the embroidered rectangle using the all-purpose thread.

8. Place the embroidered square and the remaining piece of fabric together, right sides facing. Stitch around all 4 sides, leaving a 3-inch opening along the bottom edge for turning. Clip the corners so they will lie flat after turning.

9. Turn the pillow covering right side out through the opening along the bottom edge. Stuff with the fiberfill and handstitch the turning opening closed to complete the project.

Mark the embroidery pattern on the fabric.

Full-sized embroidery pattern.

Red Roses with Yellow Daisies Tablecloth

THIS DAINTY, OLD-FASHIONED TABLE-CLOTH CAN BE MADE ANY SIZE OR SHAPE BY ADAPTING THE PATTERN. IT IS SHOWN HERE AS A SMALL TEA CLOTH TO MAKE IT EASIER TO PHOTOGRAPH. IF YOU WOULD LIKE TO MAKE A RECTANGULAR CLOTH, ADD ADDITIONAL SIDE MOTIFS ALONG THE LONG SIDES. FOR A CIRCLE, USE SIX OR EIGHT EVENLY-SPACED CORNER MOTIFS. BE SURE TO ADD LACE ACCORDINGLY IF CHANGING THE SIZE OF THE PROJECT.

DIFFICULTY LEVEL:

MATERIALS NEEDED:

- One 31-by-31-inch piece of Zweigart "Jubilee" 28-count even-weave fabric, color #1 white
- 4 yards wide flat lace
- white all-purpose thread
- 2 skeins of the following 6-strand embroidery floss:

Anchor#	DMC#		Color Name
1070	993		Jade Light
1076	991		Jade
289	307		Canary Yellow Medium Light
302	743		Citrus Medium Light
46	666		Crimson Red

FINISHED SIZE TABLECLOTH:

30 by 30 inches

MAKING THE PROJECT

Note: Three strands of the 6-strand floss are used for all embroidery.

1. Turn under 1/4-inch twice around all sides to make a doubled hem. Stitch the hem in place using the all-purpose thread.

2. Using a water-soluble pencil, transfer the embroidery designs to the fabric, spacing them 3 inches from the hemmed edges. Refer to the embroidery layout as necessary, tracing 4 corner motifs and 4 side motifs.

3. Embroider the darker stems in outline- or stem-stitch using the Jade floss. Embroider the darker leaves in single chain using the Jade floss.

4. Embroider the lighter stems and lighter leaves in Jade Light as in step 3.

5. Embroider the red roses in outline- or stem-stitch using the Crimson Red floss. Embroider the small flowers on the ends of the side motifs in lazy-daisy using the Crimson Red floss.

6. To stitch the yellow daisies, use the Canary Yellow Medium Light floss in lazy-daisy stitch. Work the centers of the roses in the same floss in outline- or stem-stitch.

7. Embroider the dots in the centers of all flowers using the Citrus Medium Light floss in French knots.

8. After completing the embroidery, attach the lace to the edges of the tablecloth to complete the project.

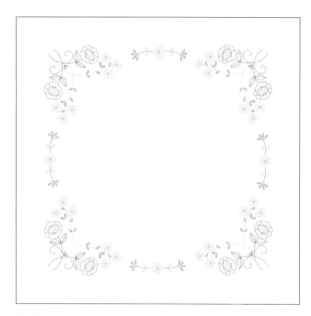

Mark the embroidery pattern on the fabric.

Full-sized side motif.

Full-sized corner motif.

Tabriz Needlepoint Cushion

Here's a needlepoint project with a detailed design—but it is not an advanced project by any means. The two major stitches used in this project are the tent-stitch and scotch-stitch.

DIFFICULTY LEVEL:

MATERIALS NEEDED:

- 14-by-14-inch square of 12-count interlocked mono canvas
- 15-by-15-inch piece of upholstery-weight fabric for backing
- 2 yards narrow gold piping (optional)
- 14-inch polyester pillow form
- 1 skein Anchor Tapisserie 20 gram grounding wool color 8004 (off-white)
- Four 3-by-15-inch strips of blue upholstery-weight fabric for borders
- Anchor Tapisserie 10m wool skeins in the following amounts and colors:

Amount	Anchor#	DMC#		Color Name
4	8220	7218		Deep Maroon
3	8630	7317		Medium Blue
2	8022	7474		Dark Gold
2	9006	7320		Medium Grass Green

FINISHED SIZE OF THE PILLOW WITH BORDERS::

14 by 14 inches

FINISHED SIZE OF CENTER SQUARE:

10 by 10 inches

MAKING THE PROJECT

1. Apply tape to the edges of the canvas to prevent the threads from catching on the edges while working.

2. Locate the center of the piece of 14-by-14-inch canvas. Begin the needlepoint at the center, following the chart. All of the stitching is done in tent stitch, with the exception of the convergence of 4 gold squares—the centers are done in off-white scotch-stitch.

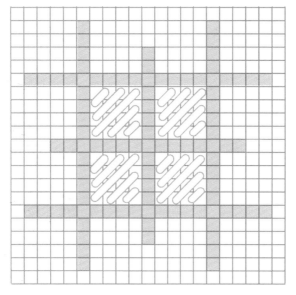

Scotch-stitch squares

3. When you have completed the needle-point, block the pillow front to eliminate the distortion that may have occurred while stitching (see chapter 7).

4. Trim the outside of the pillow front down, so that 1/2-inch of canvas extends beyond the stitched edges. This will be your seam allowance.

5. Fold the center of each blue fabric strip in half to mark the center of the borders. Stitch the borders to the center square using all-purpose thread and a 1/2-inch seam allowance. Miter the corners of the border strips and press without pressing the needlepoint area. This makes the pillow front.

6. Stitch the piping around all sides of the pillow front.

7. Stitch the pillow front and back together, right sides facing, leaving a 10-inch area open along the bottom edge for turning.

8. Clip corners and turn the pillow covering right-side out.

9. Insert the pillow form and hand-stitch the turning opening closed. This completes the project.

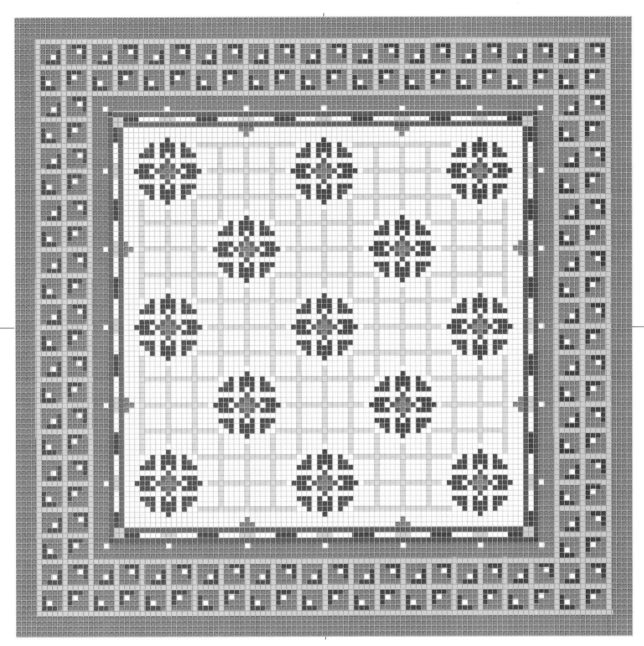

Tabriz needlepoint chart.

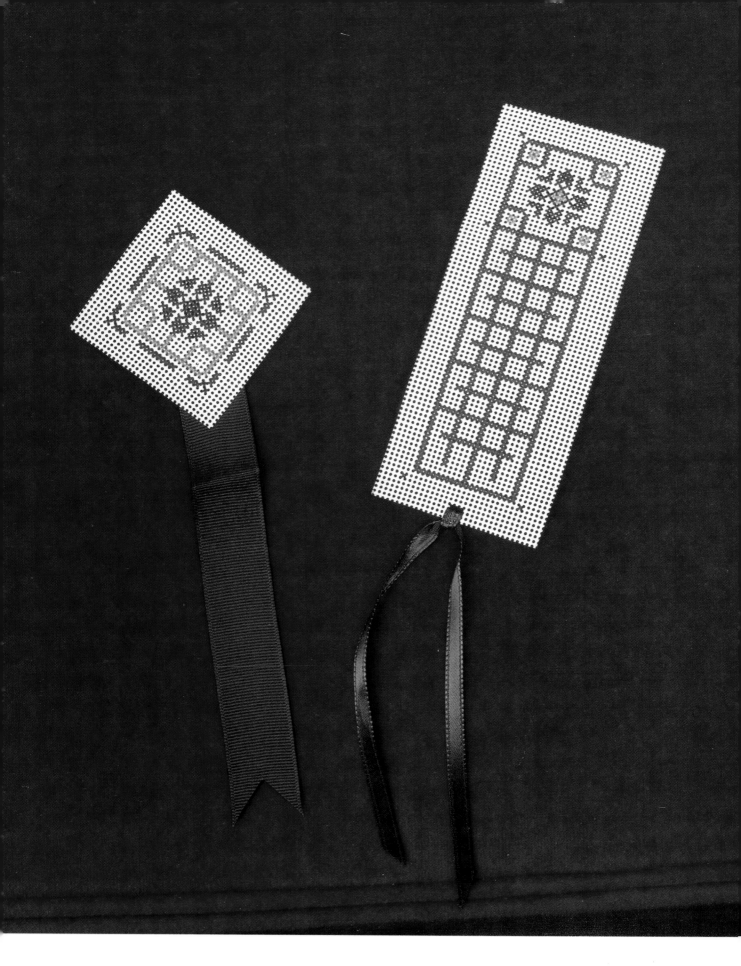

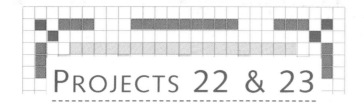

Tabriz Book Marks

I THOUGHT IT MIGHT BE FUN TO SHOW YOU HOW EASILY INTERCHANGEABLE CROSS-STITCH AND NEEDLEPOINT CAN BE! FOR THESE TWO EASY PROJECTS, I PULLED AND ADAPTED MOTIFS FROM THE TABRIZ NEEDLEPOINT PILLOW SHOWN ON THE PREVIOUS PAGES. THEN I WORKED THEM IN STRANDED FLOSS ON PERFORATED PAPER.

YOU CAN ALSO WORK THESE DESIGNS ON FABRIC, THE SQUARE DESIGN WOULD MAKE A NICE ORNAMENT OR SACHET.

DIFFICULTY LEVEL:

MATERIALS NEEDED:

- 3-by-3-inch square of 14-count perforated paper for square bookmark
- 3-by-10-inch piece of 14-count perforated paper for the rectangular bookmark
- Scraps of coordinating satin ribbon (you choose the color)
- One skein each of 6-strand embroidery floss in the following colors:

Anchor#	DMC#		Color Name
20	815		Burgundy Medium Dark
132	797		Cobalt Blue Medium Dark
890	436		Brass Light
229	700		Emerald Dark

MAKING THE PROJECTS

1. Locate the center of either of the pieces of perforated paper. Referring to their respective charts, stitch the designs on the paper working from the center outwards. Use 2 strands of floss in your needle.

2. After completing the embroidery, trim down the paper so that it extends about 1/4 inch from the stitching.

3. Trim with ribbon to complete the bookmarks. You can stitch or glue the ribbon in position.

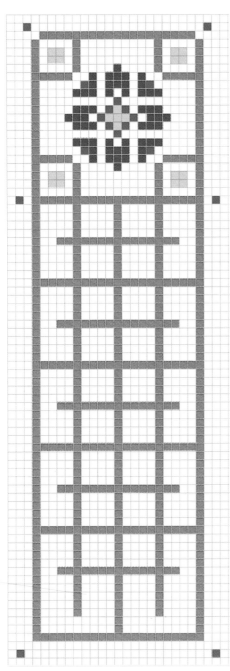

Rectangular bookmark motif.

Square bookmark motif.

Cross-Stitch Grapes Set

Tʜɪs ᴇʟᴇɢᴀɴᴛ sᴇᴛ ᴏꜰ Eᴜʀᴏᴘᴇᴀɴ-ɪɴsᴘɪʀᴇᴅ ʟɪɴᴇɴs ɪs sᴛɪᴛᴄʜᴇᴅ ᴏɴ ᴘᴜʀᴇ ʟɪɴᴇɴ ɪɴ ᴄʀᴏss sᴛɪᴛᴄʜ ᴀᴄᴄᴇɴᴛᴇᴅ ᴡɪᴛʜ sᴇʀᴘᴇɴᴛɪɴᴇ ʜᴇᴍ sᴛɪᴛᴄʜɪɴɢ. Tʜᴇ ɪɴᴛᴇʀ-ᴇsᴛɪɴɢ ʟᴏᴏᴋ ɪs ᴀᴄʜɪᴇᴠᴇᴅ ꜰʀᴏᴍ ᴜsɪɴɢ ᴛʜɪs ᴜɴᴜsᴜᴀʟ ꜰᴀʙʀɪᴄ.

Tʜᴇ ʟɪɴᴇɴ ꜰᴇᴀᴛᴜʀᴇs ᴀ ᴅɪꜰꜰᴇʀᴇɴᴛ-ᴄᴏʟᴏʀᴇᴅ ᴡᴀʀᴘ ᴀɴᴅ ᴡᴇꜰᴛ ᴛʜʀᴇᴀᴅ (ʟᴇɴɢᴛʜᴡɪsᴇ ᴀɴᴅ ᴄʀᴏssᴡɪsᴇ ᴛʜʀᴇᴀᴅs ᴏꜰ ᴛʜᴇ ꜰᴀʙʀɪᴄ). Wʜᴇɴ ʏᴏᴜ ᴘᴜʟʟ ᴏᴜᴛ ᴛʜᴇ ʟɪɢʜᴛᴇʀ-ᴄᴏʟᴏʀᴇᴅ ᴛʜʀᴇᴀᴅs ꜰᴏʀ ᴛʜᴇ ʜᴇᴍsᴛɪᴛᴄʜɪɴɢ, ᴛʜᴇ ᴅᴀʀᴋᴇʀ ᴛʜʀᴇᴀᴅs ᴀʀᴇ ʟᴇꜰᴛ ʙᴇʜɪɴᴅ—ʏᴏᴜ'ʟʟ sᴇᴇ ᴡʜᴀᴛ I ᴍᴇᴀɴ. Yᴏᴜ ᴄᴀɴ sᴜʙsᴛɪᴛᴜᴛᴇ ᴀ ʀᴇɢᴜʟᴀʀ 20-ᴄᴏᴜɴᴛ ᴇᴠᴇɴ-ᴡᴇᴀᴠᴇ ꜰᴀʙʀɪᴄ ꜰᴏʀ ᴛʜɪs ᴘʀᴏᴊᴇᴄᴛ, ʙᴜᴛ ʏᴏᴜ ᴡᴏɴ'ᴛ ɢᴇᴛ ᴛʜᴇ ɴɪꜰᴛʏ ᴛᴡᴏ-ᴛᴏɴᴇ ʀᴇsᴜʟᴛs.

Materials Needed:

- 18-by-55-inch rectangle of Zweigart 20-count "3340 Cork" Linen, color #23 for each towel (1/2 yard of fabric will make 2 towels)
- 18-by-40-inch rectangle of the same fabric for the runner
- All-purpose thread to match fabric
- Eight skeins of 6-strand embroidery floss, Anchor color #392 or DMC color #642 (linen medium)

Difficulty Level:

Making the Projects

1. For each towel, turn under 1/4 inch twice along each long side and one short side to make a doubled hem. Stitch the hem in place using the all-purpose thread.

2. For the runner, turn under and hem only the two long sides.

3. Remove a crosswise thread from the fabric 2 inches from the unhemmed short edge. Work hemstitch along the gap, taking up 2 threads per bundle. Remove the remaining crosswise threads between this line of hemstitching and the raw edge of the fabric for the fringe.

4. Remove five (5) crosswise threads from the fabric just above the fringe hemstitching. Hemstitch again along the new gap, taking up 2 threads in a serpentine pattern (refer to Chapter 8 for more information).

5. Remove a crosswise thread 4 inches from the completed serpentine band of hemstitching. Hemstitch along the gap taking up 2 threads per bundle. Remove 5 threads and hemstitch in serpentine pattern as for the previous band.

6. Locate the center of the 4-inch band, between the lines of hemstitching. Using 3 strands of floss in your needle, cross-stitch

the design inside the band, stitching across 2 threads.

7. To stitch the runner, repeat the entire procedure on both short ends of the fabric.

Serpentine Hemstitching

Serpentine Hemstitching

Fringe this end.

Hem long sides and opposite short end.

Hemstitching and embroidery placement diagram.

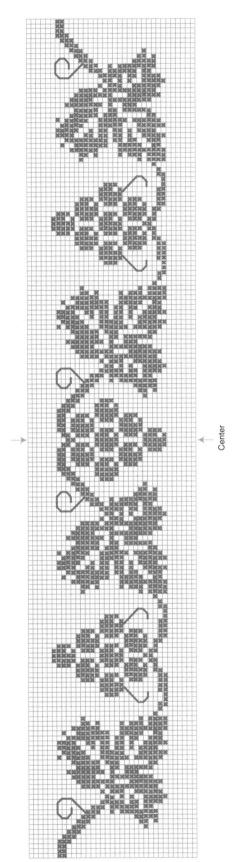

Center

Pattern for cross-stitch embroidery.

Country Rose Dresser Runner

This old-fashioned runner was inspired by a small doily found in an antiques shop. After updating the colors a bit (the original was in purple and black—yick!) and re-sizing the design, I thought it would make a nice runner. To add length to the runner, add additional lengths of the four-sided stitch.

DIFFICULTY LEVEL:

MATERIALS NEEDED:

- One 20-by-35-inch piece of Zweigart "Linda" 27-count even-weave fabric, color ivory
- Ivory all-purpose thread
- 1 skein each of the following 6-strand embroidery floss:

Anchor#	DMC#		Color Name
36	3326		Blossom Pink Light
290	972		Canary Yellow Medium
111	208		Lavender Medium Dark
265	3348		Avocado Light
228	700		Emerald Medium Dark
25	3716		Carnation Light
62	603		Magenta Medium
1035	930		Antique Blue Dark

FINISHED SIZE OF RUNNER::

18 by 28 inches

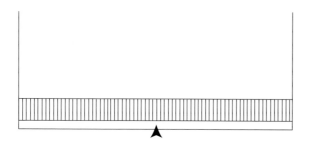

Leave several threads un-pulled near edge.
(Short ends of fabric)

Removing threads for fringe.

Mark the embroidery pattern on the fabric.

MAKING THE PROJECT

Note: Three strands of the 6-strand floss are used for all embroidery.

1. Turn under 1/4-inch twice along the two long sides to make a doubled hem. Stitch the hem in place using the all-purpose thread.

2. Remove a crosswise thread one inch from the edge of each short side. Remove the thread from this area out towards the edges, leaving 4 or 5 threads intact near the edge. Work a hemstitched fringe by taking up 4 threads (see the chapter on hem stitch for more information) and stitching with the all-purpose thread.

3. Using a water-soluble pencil, transfer the embroidery designs to the fabric, spacing them 3 inches from the hemmed and fringed edges. Refer to the embroidery layout as necessary. Add two side motifs.

4. Embroider the blue framing area in four-sided stitch using the Antique Blue Dark floss.

5. Embroider the stems in outline- or stem-stitch: use the Avocado Light floss for the lighter-colored stems and the Emerald Medium Dark for the darker ones. Embroider the solid leaves in satin-stitch, referring to the shades shown on the pattern. Embroider the 4 small leaves in single chain using the Emerald Medium Dark floss.

6. Stitch the flower outlines and petal details using the two shades of pink: Carnation Light is for the lighter flowers and Magenta Medium for the darker ones

7. Embroider the flower centers in the Canary Yellow Medium floss in clusters of French knots.

8. Stitch the lavender flowers in lazy-daisy stitch.

Side Unit

Full-sized motif

Corner Unit

Center

Full-sized corner motif.

CHAPTER 6

Collecting
and
Conservation

Finding and Purchasing Vintage Linens

Needlework—embroidery in particular—has been enjoying a revival during the past few years. Baby boomers, formerly accustomed to fast-food and fast living, are now finding themselves with a bit more time on their hands for hobbies, and are rediscovering the joys of creating or using handmade treasures in their homes.

Some of these people are stitching beautiful embroidered items themselves, while others prefer to hunt for them at antique stores, garage sales, flea markets and estate sales. Old-style linens are now hot collectibles. Once relegated to baskets and shelves at the back of the store, shops and sale tables are being picked clean of their linens by collectors yearning for a piece of the past.

Many of the die-hard collectors don't mind an occasional stain, mendable rip, or odd color combination. In fact, this adds to the charm of old linens.

Antique stores and estate sales are the most obvious places to look, but prices can be a bit high. Sometimes great pieces can be found in unexpected places such as garage sales, junk stores, second-hand stores, flea markets, church tag sales and thrift stores, and often at ridiculously low prices. I've picked up vintage table runners and doilies for as little as 25-cents apiece at garage sales, or for a dollar or two at church bazaars. Always be on the lookout for boxes stuffed under tables or linens tucked into dresser drawers.

Another useful ploy is "dropping hints" to friends and older relatives who may not care much for vintage linens. I've collected a lot of beautiful old linens using this approach. I would rather they gave them to me than see them thrown away or given to second-hand stores! I like to bake a special batch of the gift-giver's favorite cookies or bring them a pretty bouquet of flowers as a special thank-you.

If the cost of fine vintage linens is not a problem to you, seek out professional dealers and collectors of vintage pieces. Not only will you find high-quality merchandise in excellent condition, but also a person who shares your love of textiles and can give you quite a bit of advice on collecting, care, and storage. Of course, collecting the linens is the easy part—finding storage space for an ever-growing collection can be a problem. But I think I'll let you worry about storage space.

What to Look for and What to Avoid

Discovering a rack full of crisply-starched, snow-white vintage linens at the local antique store can be very exciting. But, those stiff-as-cardboard linens can also harbor problems. Heavy starch and bleaching of linens tends to damage them, and starch attracts pests.

Here are some rules of thumb for checking the linens before you purchase them:

• Is it linen or cotton? Most embroidered pieces of vintage linen are made from cotton, but you will also find many stitched on linen. A good way to tell the difference is simply by feel. Linen feels warm and a bit stiff, even without starch. Cotton feels cool and is a bit more limp or airy. Linen also holds a sharp crease better than cotton.

• Bunch the fabric tightly in your hands. Did you hear anything? Hopefully you didn't—but if you heard any snapping or crinkling, you can be sure it's from the fibers breaking. This is one of the big pitfalls of starch. It gives the fabric "body", but turns the fibers into brittle little twigs. Put that little item back on the rack.

• Hold the fabric up to a window or bright light. Are there any worn areas not easily seen without the light shining through? While some worn areas are to be expected, heavily-worn pieces should be avoided. Also avoid items which have small pin-sized holes because this is an indication of damaged fibers. Items that have been carefully mended are fine, as the mend often adds interest to the piece.

• Smell the piece. It should smell fresh or even a little old or dusty—but never musty. A

musty odor indicates moisture damage. Also avoid pieces that have been stored in plastic for long periods of time. Plastic traps moisture.
• Avoid items that smell of bleach. Unfortunately many well-meaning people attempt to clean and brighten linens by over-bleaching. But, bleach that has been applied with too heavy a concentration or has not been thoroughly rinsed from the fabric damages the item quickly. Once you get the item home and wash it, you could find it reduced to nothing more than a pile of lint.
• Stay away from curtains unless they are in absolutely impeccable condition. Items hung from windows for decades are exposed to damaging ultra-violet light and dust. They probably won't last long.
• Check for stains. This is a tough call because some stains will come out in the wash and others will not. Always avoid anything that looks like a blood or ink stain.

If you still have your heart set on a piece but it has some damage, check the price tag. Stick to items that won't break your heart (or pocketbook) if the stains won't come out during laundering, or if they fall apart after a few washings.

Tips for Using Damaged Linens

Sometimes the best buys are damaged linens. If you find a particularly interesting piece with some wear, try using it in a way other than that which it was intended.

Here are some creative ideas for using and displaying stained or worn pieces:
• Drape a tablecloth over a chair, piano, or chest. By draping the item, you can cleverly conceal the bad spots in the folds. No one will be the wiser.
• Use a handkerchief or napkin as a doily or tray cloth. Small doilies look very pretty placed between a teacup and its saucer. One of my favorite ways to display old doilies or napkins is to sandwich it between a bone china dinner plate and a clear glass salad plate.
• Stitch a new teacozy from old dresser runners, embroidered kitchen towels, doilies or tray cloths. You can use the pattern and instructions given in Chapter 5.

• Fold an embroidered runner into thirds and stitch along two sides, creating a lingerie pocket with flap. Display it on your dresser.
• Stitch small doilies from antimacassar sets (those old-time chair sets featuring a doily for the chair back and one for each arm) that are missing their mates to the fronts of ready-made pillows or cushions. Tack them in place by hand using small, invisible stitches. When you need a change, remove the doilies from the pillow and use some other ones. Rotate the supply often to keep your décor interesting and to preserve the linens.
• Drape a tablecloth over a decorative curtain rod to make an interesting, romantic valance for a bedroom. Remember that sunlight can damage and fade linens, so check it often, and try not to place them in a westward-facing window.
• Frame dainty laces and linens in a shadow box with other family treasures and trinkets for an interesting heirloom conversation piece.
• Layer smaller doilies and tray cloths over larger tablecloths for an eclectic-but-elegant table covering. Trust me, your friends will rave over it! An old embroidered bedspread makes a terrific tablecloth, too!
• Make a doll or Christening dress from the salvageable sections of a snow-white embroidered tablecloth. Add a few yards of vintage lace and you have yourself a new heirloom.
• Recycle worn-out old linens into pillows for the bedroom or stuffed animals and bears for baby's room.
• Repair holes in larger items by stitching a small doily (or salvaged pieces of doilies) over the holes. Add some vintage lace around the edges of the patch to add interest.
• Stitch small matching doilies together, trim with lace or ribbon, and stuff with potpourri for a sachet.
• Use snippets of vintage laces as napkin rings.

Linen Conservation

With a little care and consideration, your newly-made linens can become heirlooms for generations to come, and vintage linens can last a few more lifetimes. Gentle washing and drying, along with careful storage, are keys to their longevity.

To wash new linens made from modern materials, simply throw them in washing machine on the gentle cycle. Use a mild liquid soap such as Ivory Liquid® or Orvus® (available at quilting supply shops, some feed and tack stores, through textile conservators or by mail order).

To dry, larger items such as tablecloths can be placed in the clothes dryer until almost dry. Smaller items can be allowed to air-dry on a fluffy towel or sweater-drying rack.

Never allow your linens to dry completely before ironing. Damp linens simply iron better. If you iron them while they are still damp, creases have not yet had a chance to set in and are easy to remove. Plus, you won't have to wet the piece with a squirt bottle. Another benefit of damp ironing is that you can spot stains that may not have washed out of the piece completely before you set them in permanently with your hot iron! If a piece has been allowed to dry, dampen it with water, roll it in a towel and let it sit for about half an hour, until the moisture has a chance to work its way into the fibers and then iron it right away.

Washing vintage linens requires a bit more care. If an item is particularly sturdy, you can wash it in the machine as for the new linens. If it is a small item, or a bit more fragile, fill a bowl or shallow basin with room temperature water and add a tablespoon of the liquid detergent. Do not use an aluminum bowl, because this metal can react with chemicals in the detergent and make things worse. Swish with your hand to distribute the detergent evenly and then add the linens, one at a time.

Swish the linens gently—do not scrub, scrunch, bunch or wring them. If they are very dirty, allow them to sit in the soapy water for 10-15 minutes and check them. Some spots may need a little extra work, and a soft toothbrush is the perfect tool for a gentle scrub.

When the linens are clean, rinse them sev-

eral times in room-temperature water and roll in a towel to remove the excess moisture. The towel need not be rolled tightly. Once again, do not wring the linens! Textiles are the most vulnerable to damage when they are wet.

To press the damp linens, set your iron for the proper fabric setting and refer to Chapter 4 for pressing and ironing tips. Gently stretch the linen back into shape if it becomes a bit distorted during the laundering process and prepare to press.

Keep a pressing cloth handy (you can make your own by edge-finishing a piece of unbleached, lightweight cotton fabric). A pressing cloth will keep your iron from coming in contact with the item, protecting it from unintentional scorching, goop hiding on the bottom of the iron, shiny spots created by the iron, and other types of damage.

Linens and doilies with scalloped edges can be difficult to iron. To help the scallops lie flat, gently pull each scallop in several directions. Holding the tip of the scallop with a straight pin to protect your fingers, lay the press cloth over the item and iron each scallop individually, from the center outwards. Another option, one that is particularly useful for knitted or crocheted doilies, is to pin the damp items to a blocking board and allow them to dry over the course of a few days. You can find more information for this procedure in Chapter 4.

Cleaning
linens in a basin

Items that have a high relief, such as satin-stitch embroidery, French knots or padded stitches, will need to be padded before ironing to protect the stitches. The maker went through a lot of time and trouble to create those perfect stitches—don't ruin the look by flattening them like pancakes! Lay a very fluffy towel on the surface of your ironing board and place the linen face down. Cover the item with your pressing cloth and iron the piece from the backside. The fibers in the fluffy towel will protect the stitches.

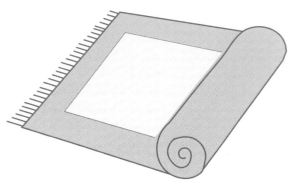

Rolling the linens in a towel to remove excess moisture.

If you are wondering why starch has not been mentioned yet, it is because I do not recommend its use until you are ready to display a piece of linen. One of the most important tips I can give you is not to starch your linens before storing them. Starching your linens before folding and storage invites damage from creases, mold, and pests.

Starch a piece only when ready to use the item. For instance, if you are having a dinner party and want to use one of your tablecloths, remove it from storage, unfold and lay flat on a clean carpet. Shut the door to keep out the kids and animals. This airs out the pieces and helps soften the creases. Next, fill a squirt bottle with a ration of 1/3 liquid laundry starch, such as Vano® and 2/3 distilled water. Shake to combine. While the piece is still lying on the floor, lightly dampen with the starch mixture. Dampen slightly more heavily along the creases, then press the item, let it cool and place immediately on the table.

Stain Removal Guide

Now we get to the part of the book that will cause the most controversy. There are as many ways of cleaning linens as there are people who clean them. Even educated conservators often bicker over proper cleaning methods!

Since most of us collect linens that are vintage (less than 100 years old), we can use stain-removal methods that may not be appropriate for fine fabrics and priceless antiques. Linens made in the last 100 years are generally very sturdy, which is why they are still around to enjoy today. Cottons and linens are easy to clean—polyester-blend items often have permanent stains.

The best way to tackle new stains is to treat them as soon as they occur. Never throw soiled linens or tablecloths in the clothes hamper until washday. This will allow the stains to dry and set, making them difficult—if not impossible—to remove.

Linens that are simply dusty can be vacuumed to clean them. Remove the tool from the end of the vacuum hose. To prevent the item from being sucked into the vacuum, place a doubled length of pantyhose on the end of the hose. Knee-highs are great for this purpose. If you are able to adjust your vacuum for less suction, do this too.

To remove iron-based stains, such as rust, blood or anything that looks like rust, first clean the item in the traditional method to see if you can remove or reduce the stain. If it is still there you can remove it by applying an iron-stain remover such as Whink® (available at the grocery store in the laundry aisle) to a cotton swab and gently cleaning the stain only. Rinse immediately several times in room temperature running water.

Do not allow the chemical to sit and soak for any reason. If the stain does not come out during the first treatment, repeat the procedure as many times as it takes to get the stain out, rinsing thoroughly each time you apply the chemical.

Candle wax can be removed by first gently scraping the excess wax from the fabric using a plastic spatula. Remove as much of the wax as possible. Then, sandwich the wax-laden portion of the item between paper towels and press with a hot iron. The paper towels will absorb the melting wax. Change the paper towels frequently so you do not redistribute the wax back to the linen.

Coffee and tea stains or those from *wine* should be treated as soon as they happen. One of the recommended methods is to pour boiling water from a teakettle directly through the stain. To do this, place the piece over a colander in the sink before pouring the water. Then, give the item a 10-minute soak in warm water with a bit of mild detergent and wash as usual. Some people insist that pouring white wine through a red wine stain will clean it. Personally I have never tried this, but it might be worth a look.

Use the same method used in the previous paragraph for grease or gravy stains, but first rub a little bit of mild liquid soap into the stain. If the stain is a persistent one, try rubbing the area with a mixture of salt and lemon juice and then wash the item.

The yellowing caused by age can often be removed by soaking the items in warm water to which a few tablespoons of baking soda have been added. Soak for an hour and check the items. If they are still yellowed, soak a bit longer. You can also try an old-time trick that actually works very well—lay the dampened cloth on a clean white sheet out in the sunshine and let Mother Nature remove the yellowing for you.

I don't advocate the use of bleach unless there is no other way to remove a stain, and only when treating white fabrics. Bleaches can cause yellow stains all their own, which are impossible to remove. Never use bleach on the colored embroidery threads.

To try removing a stain using a bleach solution, use a ration of 1 part chlorine bleach to 5 parts water. Using an old white washcloth for large areas or a cotton swab for smaller areas, gently dab the solution on the stain. Wait 5 minutes and launder the item. You may need to repeat the process a few more times to get the stain out. Non-chlorine bleach used in the same manner will help remove stains from colored items or near the colored embroidery threads.

Storing Fine Linens

First and foremost, linens must be completely dry before storing. Clean, starch-free linens should be wrapped in acid-free tissue for storage and stored in archival boxes or lined cupboards and drawers. They can also be stored in bags made from fabric. The cupboard and drawer liners and fabric bags should be made from unbleached 100% cotton fabric.

Acid-free tissue and archival boxes are available through conservators, or at businesses that supply materials for artists and photographers, and at some stationers. Unbleached cotton is available at any fabric store, but before using it, wash it to remove any coatings applied during the manufacturing process.

Larger linens can also be folded into strips and hung from hangers in a closet. Line the bar of the hanger with unbleached cotton. Another method for storing large linens is to wrap them around a shipping tube or a wide piece of PVC piping which have been covered with unbleached cotton. You can stand these up in a corner of a closet. Both of these methods help reduce the damage caused by creases—but do refold the items now and then.

Air your linens regularly. Remove and refold the linens now and then to avoid damage caused by creasing. Not only does this help make the linens last longer, it is also a great way to revisit your collection.

Never store linens in plastic or directly on a wood surface, even if has been sealed or varnished. Plastic traps moisture and allows mildew to form. Wood surfaces—even sealed ones—can cause a chemical reaction, which can cause a terribly permanent stain to form on the fabric.

But whatever storage method you choose, do enjoy your linens. You should not be afraid to pull them out and use them. Why else would you collect them?

Retail Supply Sources

The following resources will help you locate specific materials used in this book, if you are unable to find them locally. Many have toll-free order numbers, Web sites and catalogs. Contact the sources for more information.

Herrschners
www.herrschners.com
2800 Hoover Road
Stevens Point, WI 54492
(800) 713-1239

Craftsmen's Studio
www.craftsmensstudio.com
27 Ring Road
Greensboro, NC 27405
(800) 234-2808

The Needlepoint Joint
www.needlepointjoint.com
241 Historic 25th Street
Ogden, UT 84401
(801) 394-4355

Knight's Thread Express
www.threadexpress.com
75 McIntire Road
New Gloucester, ME 04260
(888) 826-1519

Stitcher's Paradise
www.stitchers-paradise.com
8064 Skyway
Paradise, CA 95969
(530) 877-9195

The Scarlet Letter
www.scarlet-letter.com
P.O. Box 397
Sullivan, WI 53178
(414) 593-8470

Lacis
www.lacis.com
3163 Adeline Street
Berkeley, CA 94703
(510) 843-7178

Metric Equivalent Conversion Chart

Here's a practical method for converting from US measure to Metric using a calculator, for our stitching friends abroad:

To Convert From US	To Metric	Multiply By
inches	centimeters	2.540
inches	millimeters	25.40
square inches	square centimeters	6.452
square inches	square millimeters	645.2
feet	meters	0.3048
square feet	square meters	0.09290
yards	meters	0.9144
square yards	square meters	0.08361